Once in a Lullaby

Once in a Lullaby

My Journey Home

C.L. Burger

To: A. E. K. and H.

I dedicate this book to you my dear granddaughters. I encourage you to be truthful and caring, yet strong in your boundaries. Be the best person you can be. I hope and pray the words shared with you here will create an inheritance that is invaluable, even if it is only the lessons your Grandma has learned on her life journey. Always believe you can reach your heart's desire.

With all my love,
Grandma Cindy

Contents

Foreword

*R*ecently I was struck by the realization that the people I most admire and value in my life have often experienced a great deal of adversity as children. Despite the early adversity, their resilience shines through. Cindy Burger is one of those people.

I met Cindy when she was director of a homeless ministry and I was a new employee of another agency seeking to serve the city's homeless population. From the moment I first introduced myself, I recognized in Cindy many of the qualities illustrated in her story—compassion, determination, kindness, and protectiveness, not just for herself but also for the individuals she was serving. I knew the moment we met that it would take repeated action on my part, not words, to win her trust.

Over the course of several months, we built that trust and became friends. We connected with each other and we connected through our shared passion for serving individuals who were homeless.

Cindy and I had another thing in common. We had both been CASA volunteers—specially trained court appointed advocates who speak up on behalf of a child in foster care. When I later became the Executive Director of the local CASA program, Cindy was an early source of strong support. She has been an exemplary ambassador of the power of connection and advocacy to serve the best interests of a child who has been abused or neglected. We both place a high priority on healing and building resilience in children as early as possible.

Which brings me back to the people I've known with a high degree of resilience. They move through the world with both a genuine joy to connect and a healthy skepticism that things are not always what they seem. They make great teachers, based on lessons learned from a life journey that has not always been smooth and easy. The story you are about to read offers a rare glimpse at the journey that one determined and stubborn woman took to develop that resilience in herself, so that she might also share that gift with the world. As one who has seen this gift at work, I thank Cindy, for her courage to begin the journey, her perseverance to see it through and her generosity in sharing the story with all of us.

Tracy L. Fauver, LCSW

Introduction

My career in a nonprofit homeless ministry came to a rather abrupt end in 2013. After that, I enjoyed caring for grandbabies and working part-time in a delightful gift shop in my small town. Yet I still longed for what many spiritual directors refer to as "the more."

That is what I wanted. I wanted "the more." I asked, "Lord, what are you calling me to now?" That evening, I had the following dream:

I am walking in an orchard toward an old barn. As I approach the barn, I see my friend Martha Moore out in the orchard. She has just returned from work. She is dancing around the trees exclaiming how much she loves her job. As I watch her, I feel a deep longing in my soul and spirit to be more like Martha. (Note: More/Moore) The barn is open and I see hay bales inside. As I approach the barn, the hay bales glow in a golden light. The message from the light told me that what I am approaching will shine like gold for more than just my immediate circle of family and friends. Behind the barn, there is a group of Sisters of Mercy. (At one point in my life, I had been an associate with the Sisters of Mercy, a religious organization of Catholic nuns.) Many of the sisters are old and wise, and I had a sense that time was running out. The sisters are dressed in Hare Krishna robes and gathered in a prayer circle. I thought that was quite strange.

I woke up and "Hare Krishna" was stuck in my mind.

My faith background is, and always has been, Christian. I identified more with the Sisters of Mercy in this dream but was confused by what they were wearing. I was clueless about the meaning of Hare Krishna and could not get back to sleep until I looked up the definition for the words. This is what I found on the home page for Hare Krishna: "Krishna is a name of the Supreme. It means 'all-attractive.' Anything that might attract you has its source in the Supreme." Hare (pronounced huh-ray) is a call to Krishna's divine energy (or the highest calling.)[1]

Then I received this leading and direction from God:

Time is running out. You must be more like Martha. (See biblical reference Luke 10:38-40.) Take action and write your book. It is My/your highest calling. The book will be gold for many as it speaks of my love, grace, and mercy.

My prayer, dear granddaughters and other readers, is that you are blessed as you discover the gold God has for you here.

1

Life Begins at Seven

My life began when I was seven years old. My sister Gayle and I lived in a few foster homes by the time we arrived at our new home in the summer of 1960. We assumed this placement was just another brief stop on the way to a long line of foster homes. We didn't care about this home. In fact, we didn't care about much at all. We had already learned that caring...hurts.

Foster care toughens a kid because it is a life of survival of the fittest. You never know what will happen next. Some would say I am feisty. I admit I was a stubborn child. Today, my son and daughter will tell you that my stubborn trait grew stronger when I became their mother.

More than once in my life, tenacity kept me alive and got me places I never thought I would go. Stubbornness was also a shadow side of my personality that created challenges later in life. Tenacity for the sake of persevering can be a good trait to have. However, having a stubborn streak while also being in the wrong is a tough lesson to learn.

I was quite proud of my stubbornness during my foster home years. They frequently served oatmeal for breakfast and I hated oatmeal! The fight over oatmeal happened every morning and the battle line was drawn. "You will eat your oatmeal or sit at the table until you do!" All the other children went outside to play, while I sat in front of a cold, sticky pile of oatmeal that got colder by the minute. I sat and sat and sat…until it was almost time for dinner. I was determined not to eat that oatmeal which only frustrated the adults more. I refused to cooperate and simply waited them out. I was in college before I decided an occasional bowl of oatmeal wasn't such a bad thing.

I didn't know much about my birth mother at the time. I only knew that I waited every day for her to visit us at the foster homes, and she never showed up. That hope and want repeatedly dashed messed up my self-esteem. I believed at the core of my being that I was not worth visiting or not loved enough to "come for." I found out later that my birth mother was an alcoholic and drug addict. She may have wanted to visit us as she promised, but her addiction (or incarcerations due to her addiction) prevented her from doing so.

Before we were adopted, I remember watching our new foster dad as he sat in his hospital bed in the family room searching through piles of phone books (written copies of phone numbers of every person in a specific area of the country.) I watched as he carefully scanned each page, sometimes using a magnifying glass to double check a name. I later found out he was looking for our birth father because a birth parent must give written legal permission before a child can be adopted. Dad spent many long hours looking through the Southern California phone books until he eventually found the phone number for our birth father.

2

The Visitors and New Life

Our birth father came to visit us one day at our new foster home, and Gayle stood with her arm stretched out in front of me. If she were a lion, she would have roared. Instead, she jutted her chin up in the air and glared at him. She was not going to let him get too close. Gayle took her "older sister job" seriously throughout our lives because it was her job to take care of me and quite often tell me what to do and how to do it. By the grace of God, we were able to stay together in foster care. Not all foster children are so fortunate.

Our birth father brought each of us a wristwatch draped around a Disney princess statue. Mine was Cinderella and Gayle's was Snow White. I cherished that watch and ceramic statue and felt genuinely cared about. I knew somewhere deep inside, that this gift or more importantly the giver of the gift was very special. At the time, I didn't know how great the sacrifice was that came with that gift. The visit by the "watch man" as I called him then, was my birth father arriving to sign an agreement to give up his rights as our father.

Our birth mother also came to visit but didn't come to the house. We visited her in the park next to the courthouse where I shivered on a cold metal bench, carefully holding the doll she gave me. The doll had moving parts. The head, neck, arms and legs, and even the hands moved. Toys were not as advanced as they are today, and the doll had cracks at all the parts that moved. I remember staring at that doll and thinking, *This doll is broken all over...just like me.*

After that visit, the only reminder of my birth parents was my Cinderella watch and the doll that was broken in lots of places. It seemed as quickly as they visited, they just as quickly disappeared from our lives.

Not long after the visitors, we waited while our foster parents went through the adoption process. I was afraid of the judge in his black robe. I don't remember doing more than nodding my head or whispering yes, and we were adopted. On a hot June day in 1961, one day before Gayle's ninth birthday and just after my seventh birthday...my life began.

3

Roots

1 am not certain how many foster homes Gayle and I were in before our adoption. I remember at least two. It's difficult to describe our foster home experiences. I guess you could say it feels more like screen shots in a movie…a flashback to memories of wearing shoes too small and the reason for my bunions today. I remember a little dog that barked too much, two older girls in one of the homes, and more oatmeal I refused to eat. We moved from place to place, never staying long enough to set down any roots.

Child Development experts consider the years prior to the age of seven as the "magical thinking" years. The thought process causes them to think or believe they are (magically) the cause for things happening.[2] It makes sense that every time we left a foster home I believed that I caused us to leave. Each time we left a home, I believed I was not worth keeping. When I was old enough to comprehend that my birth parents gave us away I thought, *I must be so horrible, not even my own parents want to keep me.* Today I know that is not true. However, at the age of seven it was difficult to make sense of it in any other way. It is no surprise that my roots were quite fragile in 1961.

Our new Mom and Dad helped us establish roots and I am grateful they adopted us. I am also grateful to my sister,

Betty Jo, for putting up with two bratty little kids when she was sixteen years old. I suppose I should speak for myself when I say we were bratty. I am not sure Gayle would appreciate me speaking for her.

Our new home was unique. Our adoptive father had been in a wheelchair for most of his adult life. He had been struck with Transverse Myelitis, an inflammation of the spinal cord, while serving in the army during WWII. I often watched him work or read or make telephone calls from his hospital bed and thought of it as his command center. I figured I could easily out run and out maneuver this man in the wheelchair. Then one day I mouthed off to him and he practically took his wheelchair airborne to catch me! From that moment on, I never under estimated what he was capable of accomplishing.

Our adoptive mother was an army nurse and then a school nurse. Betty Jo was their natural daughter and so beautiful I thought she must be a model or a princess. This new family was lifesaving.

I am an introvert and usually observe more than I participate or join in. Being an observer when I was young was a way for me to protect myself or remain guarded from other people.

I watched my new dad more than I realized over the years. He was one of the first disabled people to have his car modified so he could drive. He did almost everything anyone else could do and that impressed me. In fact, he was the best ping-pong player I have ever known and won almost every game we played. I say almost, because I am certain he felt sorry for me and threw a game or two so I could win occasionally. He never let his physical challenge stop him or get in his way and I admired his determination.

Years of birthday parties, sleepovers, Girl Scouts, art classes, and plenty of outdoor play drove my roots deeper. A mulberry tree stood tall in the backyard and every summer we played house under that tree. Teacups, saucers, and even a little broom filled our wooden cupboard. I spent many Saturdays under that tree, sweeping the dirt, putting away toy dishes, and serving the neighbor kids at the table we set up in the shade. We drank juice in those little teacups, ate peanut butter and jelly sandwiches, and laughed and played until the sun went down.

We lived in a sprawling ranch home with a barn and pasture where Betty Jo took care of her horses. All around us were fig orchards and a canal where we caught frogs and tadpoles. A thick rope dangled from a large fig tree next to the canal so we could swing out over the edge and drop into the cool water during the sweltering Central Valley summers. All in all, life was good. Our new mom was a strict but loving mother. We learned how to sew, cook and clean, and all the other chores that most "good girls" needed to learn back in the day.

Only a handful of careers were socially acceptable for women. Our mom was a nurse, and Gayle and I became teachers. I have to admit I often dreamed of becoming a lawyer, but few women dared to consider such a thing. I took piles of books out in the back yard and read for hours at a time. I am proud to say I read every Nancy Drew book in the series. As I got older, I could not find enough mystery or psychology books to satisfy my hunger for reading.

Our life as adopted children was rich in many ways. We took road trips to a variety of places including Alaska and Canada and our grandmother's home in Washington. Those trips were long and challenging because we got up at 3:00 a.m. It was much cooler traveling before the sun came up, especially in the summer. One summer our parents took cantaloupe up to Washington, and I got carsick smelling the ripening melons in the car. I ate junk food to try to settle my stomach. Unfortunately, as my new parents tried to warn me, that remedy did not work at all!

I loved our visits to Grandma's house. As soon as we arrived, Gayle and I ran all the way up her stairs to jump on the feather bed. We watched our cousins kill slugs and snails with salt. As sadistic as it sounds, we marveled at the effect salt had on those little creatures. Not a pretty sight, but nonetheless fascinating to the curious little kids we were at the time. My grandmother and I sat on her back porch snapping beans as we inhaled the wonderful fragrance of the sweet peas that grew in her garden. Today the fragrance of sweet peas reminds me of our visits with Grandma.

One of the other important things we learned in our new home was growing in our relationship with God. We attended church on a regular basis and played in the bell choir and even taught Sunday school when we were older.

Some people do not care to learn about faith. I just know that my life would have been much more difficult if I did not have a solid faith foundation. I am grateful I learned early on what it means to be a true disciple of Jesus Christ. By that I don't mean someone who just warms a pew on Sunday and then becomes a Monday morning atheist. I am talking about a true follower of Christ who lives like Jesus taught us to live. The best explanation for my deep passion for the Christian faith can be summed up by the words of Mother Teresa, "I love all faith traditions, but I'm in love with mine."[3]

4

Love

*L*ove was an odd and tricky thing to me as a young girl. I suppose I was ambivalent about love, but I noticed the love my parents had for each other. My dad was what I call a "stoic German." There was not much open affection shown, but he made sure he bought our mom gifts she would enjoy on her birthday and other special occasions.

I loved helping my dad buy jewelry for my mom. This was no easy task for someone in a wheelchair in the 1960s. Driving a car as a physically challenged person was quite the miracle. Self-driving cars did not exist at that time, and anyone who drove had to be able to move their feet in order to use the brake and gas pedals. Of course, my dad was not able to do that. He did not let that stop him though. Dad had his Cadillac rigged with hand brakes and gas pedal. He pulled himself into the car using a rod installed over the front seat and then pulled his legs in and adjusted his body as needed. He was an excellent driver and I felt safe in the car with him.

Dad always took one of his daughters with him to help him pick out jewelry. I am amazed as I think about the trust the jeweler had in Dad and the confidence Dad had in us. It was strenuous for him to get in and out of the car. He usually called the jeweler ahead of time and let him know exactly what he wanted and told the jeweler that Gayle or I would come into the store to get the jewelry. In the meantime, the jeweler selected several rings, bracelets, and earrings for Dad to look at. I was stunned as the jeweler placed diamonds, rubies, and pearls in my hand to take out to Dad in the parking lot. He looked at them and made a decision or chose one and called the jeweler later to tell him how he would like it changed or adjusted. He was meticulous in choosing just the right design, and the jeweler was more than willing to help Dad select the perfect jewelry gift for our mom. Today, there is absolutely no way a jeweler would allow someone to shop like that! An adult, much less a child, would not be safe carrying such valuables out to a parking lot. Dad's careful selection of the perfect gift showed love in ways that words could not express. The care and time he took in choosing the perfect gift, spoke volumes to me about love.

Although my dad was careful in the gifts he selected, he could also be gruff with Mom. I winced when he said something cruel or belittled her in front of company. I think that said more about the male-dominated society of the times. Women are still treated as second-class citizens in spite of the many gains we have made over the decades. There certainly was not much of a voice for women in the 1960s and most men treated women with very little respect.

I had a few crushes as a young girl. One crush I will always remember is a boy named George. He was Catholic and from a large family. Because of that, he had two middle names and I liked to call him by his full name. I was in junior high school at the time, and even though I had known him since second grade, he didn't become my heartthrob until I was twelve or thirteen.

George reminded me of Elvis Presley, my true heartthrob. He wore a black leather jacket that smelled like Marlboro cigarettes. His black hair fell over one eye or was greased back when he wanted to impress a girl. He was definitely not the kind of guy my parents expected me to hang out with, but maybe that's why I was so attracted to him. His crystal blue-green eyes melted me into a puddle every time he looked at me. He always called me by my full name too (not something I allowed many people to do) and when he said "Cynthia," my knees buckled and I stuttered when I tried to respond. Eventually, George and I moved on with our lives, but he always held a special place in my heart. I gave up on George when a girl from my high school freshman class followed him around and took over his life so he could not pay attention to his ex-girlfriends. Some years later when I was in college, a mutual friend saw him working in a leather store, and George bought a purse and asked her to give it to me. He told her he had never forgotten me. A few years after that I got a letter from him. He sent me his stripes from his uniform when he enlisted in the military and said he hoped I would always remember him. I am a hopeless romantic and still have those stripes somewhere in the garage.

There was a definite pattern in the boys I liked. I alternated, it seemed, between the "boy next door" and the "bad boy" type. It was not until much later in my life that I realized why that pattern had developed. Other boyfriends did not stand out much except for one. He was a senior and I was a sophomore in high school when we started dating. He was trouble on campus, and all the guys gathered in the school parking lot and hung around his Model-A truck that he rebuilt. Every "cool kid" wanted to hang out with him.

Of course, the one time I decided to break my parents' rules and leave campus at lunch, I got into a car accident in his truck. My boyfriend took a corner too fast and suddenly his brakes locked, and before I knew it, the truck flipped over and landed with the hood of the car resting on the curb.

He was in the gutter underneath it. There were three of us in the truck and I was in the middle. I was pretty banged up but managed to walk back to the campus since the accident happened near the school. When I finally gathered the courage to tell my parents what happened, mainly because I was in a great deal of pain, my mom took me to the doctor and found out I had a cracked rib. I don't think I ever broke any of my parents' rules after that. My relationship with that boyfriend did not last long. I felt sorry for him in the hospital and called only to hear him flirting with the nurses. He thought it was great to have all those women taking care of him. I was not impressed so I broke up with him and that was the end of that.

My dating pattern turned around again, and I met Dennis when he was a senior in high school and I was a junior. He was the epitome of the "boy next door" and even resembled a popular wholesome kid on a television show called *Andy Griffith*. He looked a lot like the main character played by the actor Ron Howard. He was most definitely the perfect guy all the way around. Without even realizing it, I knew I could fade into the background whenever he was near because no one who met him would notice me. That is exactly what I needed in my life…to fade into the background. I felt safer if I could hide.

5

Swept Up and the Early Years

D ennis and I married in June of 1975. The early years of our marriage focused on getting through college and moving from place to place. We moved from California to West Virginia, where Dennis was born, so he could get his master's degree. I got my bachelor's degree and a teaching credential while he completed his master's.

I loved the people and fall colors of West Virginia, but I am a born and raised California girl and did not like the cold winters. One day I climbed a snowy hill to take the rapid transit system to the campus. I felt like a block of ice in the transit car and realized that even the ink in my pen had frozen solid.

We lived on a tight budget in an apartment complex that regularly smelled like curry. The apartment we lived in had just two rooms and a small bathroom. Yet like most young married couples, we managed to make ends meet and still enjoy life. We moved back to California shortly after Dennis completed his master's degree.

I repeated my teacher training because California did not have reciprocity with West Virginia. Dennis had a master's degree and had started on his PhD by the time my schooling was done. I completed almost as many units for my bachelor's degree as Dennis had for his master's, so I had no interest in more schooling at that point. Much later, I told Dennis I wanted to go back to school to get my counseling degree, but he discouraged me from pursuing that goal. He said people would call me at home and that would interfere with our lives.

Dennis continued with his PhD while I worked as an instructional aid in a special education class and went to school for my California teacher credential. I found out I was pregnant the same day I signed my contract for my first teaching job. It was a rough first trimester of morning sickness and full-time teaching.

I loved my job and especially the students. My first year of teaching allowed me to find my passion. I should say compassion. Most of my students struggled in a variety of ways, but I think the majority were living in poverty and others lived in abusive homes.

I will never forget the day one of my students refused to complete his homework for the fourth time. He could barely read as a senior in high school. He was a big guy, probably weighing over 300 pounds and was quite threatening to students and school staff. He shuffled his feet down the school hallways and everyone called him "the steamroller." I told him I would have to call his home to talk to his parents because he had not done his homework again.

He glared at me through squinted eyes as he mumbled, "We don't have a phone."

"Then I will make a home visit."

He stopped in his tracks and stared hard at me. He shuffled toward me and pressed his fists into the top of my desk. He got so close, I could feel his hot breath on my face when he growled, "If you do that…I will have to kill you!"

To this day, I don't know how I managed it, but I looked him straight in the eye and said with every ounce of toughness I could summon, "Well, that's just a chance I'll have to take!"

He threw his head back, laughed, and left the classroom slamming the metal double door behind him. It took me about a week to breathe again!

That student warmed up to me after that encounter. He said he wanted to learn how to drive, and I eventually taught him how to read and spell by using a driver's education manual. He could finally read well enough to pass his written test for his license. After that, he was always there if I needed any help in my classroom. One day I asked him to help me move a large table. He gave me a broad grin and lumbered over to the table. With very little effort, he put one hand underneath it, lifted it high in the air and carried it across the room dropping it into place with a loud thud. He became one of my favorite students. Although I didn't know it at the time, he and I would cross paths again several years later.

I completed most of my first year of teaching until William was born at the end of April. Shortly after that, we packed up and moved again. Most universities have an unwritten rule that in order to be on their faculty, you need to go away and become an expert in your field. Dennis decided we would move to Texas. Actually, it was almost to Mexico. His new job was at a citrus center at the very southern tip of Texas in the Rio Grande Valley. As I packed our belongings, I watched the news of the enormous Hurricane Allen. It filled the entire Gulf of Mexico and that was where we were moving! I felt sick to my stomach at the thought of moving so far away from family, but we went because Dennis' career was the priority. It is accurate to say I remained sick to my stomach almost the entire time we lived in Texas.

6

A Foreign Land

*L*ife in Texas was undeniably a culture shock. As I said, I am a born and raised California girl. California was farther ahead than most states when it came to women's rights in the early 1980s. I spent some of my years in California in leadership positions with the American Association of University Women (AAUW). I also lived in a politically liberal California city before we moved.

The first newspaper headline I read in Texas was the vote of the school board to decide whether male teachers could go to work without a tie and if it was okay for them to grow a beard. School authorities making such personal decisions was quite unfamiliar to me. Like Dorothy from the *Wizard of Oz*, I was certain I had dropped into the middle of a strange land.

Fortunately, we had company in our more liberal way of thinking. We soon became friends with another couple who moved from California to Texas five years before us. They helped us maneuver the conservative politics, the humidity, and the giant creeping things we found in our home. When they say everything in Texas is bigger, that includes the spiders! In fact, I remember when we drove to Texas in our little VW Rabbit, I refused to get out of the car to switch drivers. The tarantulas were so big they were visible from the car as they crawled across the freeway. There was no way I was going to get near one of those things! I preferred several bruises from scooting over the gearshift, rather than risk assault by a Texas-sized spider or scorpion. The drive through Texas on our way to our destination at the southern tip of the state took longer than any other road trip I had ever taken in my entire life.

Louise was born two years after we moved to Texas. Taking care of my children was my lifesaver. There were days I did not want to leave the house in the summer due to the unbearable humidity. In fact, in the last months of my pregnancy, I did not leave the house much at all. It was a horrible feeling to walk outside and be dripping in perspiration before I even got into the car. I was mostly at home and in the house the entire three years we lived there. I have never been as grateful for air conditioning as I was in south Texas.

We were the minority in this primarily Hispanic town. The racist and bigoted opinions of other white people I met frequently caused my jaw to drop. One time a sweet, southern accented woman referred to the Brazil nuts in the bowl on the table as "nigger toes." I was so shocked I didn't say another word for the rest of the evening. I never encountered such blatant racism in all my life! I either was extremely naïve or moving from a liberal California city to a more conservative town in the southern tip of Texas was more of a shock than I expected.

I can be quite stubborn when it comes to social justice. I dig my heels in when I sense someone trying to force me to comply with their way of thinking. I have strong feelings about any injustice and can find myself in situations where I must speak my mind. I began to speak my mind more and more over the three years we lived in Texas.

Women in general, and in Texas in particular, were expected (by men and many southern women) to be quiet and demure and to passively agree no matter what. That is not who I am or ever wanted to be. In hindsight, I saw myself as a bit of a rebel. The truth is I stifled my opinion for many years. I had a voice; I learned to suppress it because that was the way things were for women in those days. Today I wonder what impact I could have had in the world if I had viewed my perceived rebellion more as a power for change, rather than something to be stifled.

I was a young mother of two small children and loved taking care of them. However, there comes a point when young mothers (and fathers) have memorized all the toddler songs and are humming them in the shower. That is the time to find more academic or adult company if only for the sake of personal sanity! I wanted adult conversation about politics and world news and assumed I could find some like-minded people at the Women's Political Caucus meeting.

The minute I stepped into the room, everyone fell silent and stared at me. That's when I realized I was the only white woman in the room. Apparently, there were two Women's Political Caucus meetings. One on one side of the tracks (the railroad tracks divided the town) and one on the other side of the tracks. The one I attended was for the Hispanic women. The meeting for the white women in the community was taking place on the other side of the tracks.

The women were cordial but asked me afterwards if I knew there was another meeting elsewhere. They did not want me to feel uncomfortable. I said I was fine attending their meeting if they would have me. I think my lack of being offended and the courage they assumed I had in "crossing the tracks," caused them to welcome me even more. The white women ostracized me after that, and you would have thought I had committed the gravest of sins by attending the meeting on the other side of the tracks. I don't think I realized it, but I felt a sense of comradery with the Hispanic women and the blatant, ugly racial prejudice in the white women made this land feel even more foreign.

My liberal politics and view of life created more waves in the community. Longing for adult friends, I started a branch of the American Association of University Women in that small town. No one in that community had organized educated women before, so it was an odd thing for the city council to comprehend. As I look back on it, the all-male city council most likely felt threatened by any group of organized women. Word spread quickly in this small community about the "liberal woman from California."

I attended the school board meeting to suggest a thing called job sharing and presented the option because a friend of mine also wanted to teach part-time. I explained how it could easily work. They asked me where I got such an idea, and I told them that job sharing was common in California where I was from. A cold silence fell over the room. The president of the school board ever so slowly picked up my written proposal and drawled just as slowly, "Oh…Y'all are from C-A-L-I-FORNIAAH," as if my home state was some diseased place! He quite noticeably picked up the proposal between his thumb and forefinger like it carried some type of plague and dropped it in the nearest trash can as he drawled in disgust, "We can't have thaaaat."

In the meantime, our local branch of AAUW grew in membership, and the Texas state organization recognized us with an award. Surprisingly, the city council also acknowledged our growth and community participation. The news of our award was to be announced in the local newspaper.

The reporter from the paper was about eighty years old and met me at the library for my interview. After she asked enough questions for her story, she wanted to know what my husband's name was. I frowned and didn't answer. She put her pen down and waited.

"Why do you need to know my husband's name?"

She lifted her chin up in the air. "We always use the husband's name when a woman does something newsworthy." I clenched my jaw. "My name is Cindy." She ruffled a bit and asked me again what my husband's name was. I was determined not to tolerate discrimination in any form. When she asked me a third time, I smiled and leaned in with a wicked grin and whispered, "Which husband?" She dropped her pen and with a gasping "thank you," ran out of the room. The next day, the article about the new Texas Branch of the American Association of University Women reported the president's name was Cindy Burger.

My tenacity came out in other ways too. Our experience when William was born in a small town in California was wonderful. He was born in a birthing room with no bright lights or stark white walls like the delivery room. His entry into the world, albeit after more than twenty-four hours of labor, was a calm entry in a birthing room with soft music and dim lights. We were determined to have a similar delivery when our next baby was born two years later.

The obstetrician we saw in Texas was a funny old guy. He said he had given up on determining the sex of babies before they were born because he was wrong so many times. When I had my children, hospitals were not equipped with the type of medical equipment that could reveal the gender of the baby before birth. It was all guesswork. In fact, after one of my appointments, the doctor told me I was either going to have a calm girl or a hyperactive boy. William was such an active two-year-old, I remember praying (obviously after the fact) "Please God, let it be a calm girl!"

The rule in this Texas hospital was you must have a delivery room birth. There would be none of the soft lights and frou-frou birth methods like "liberal California." The tough foster child in me bucked the system. I didn't like rules and never had. It didn't matter one way or the other to our doctor, but we must follow the rules of the hospital.

We discussed our plan for the hospital trip, and Dennis told me he could not function well at night, and if possible, he would prefer that I have this baby during the day. I was so co-dependent, I waited until I was in the transition phase of birth before I woke him up to tell him we really needed to get to the hospital now! I can tell you from experience, the best way to forget all about your labor pains is to keep your eyes four feet from the back of a semi-truck on the freeway. Dennis was driving so fast on the way to the hospital, I was sure I would die splatted on the back of that truck.

When we arrived, an orderly saw me bent over as I got out of the car. He quickly shoved an old woman out of a wheelchair in the parking lot, put me in the chair and rushed me upstairs. He was there at just the right time. Otherwise, Louise would have been born on the front lawn of that hospital!

There was no time to move me to the delivery room. I was already in full labor. My doctor came in, removed his mask and with a big grin said, "That's a pretty sneaky way to avoid a delivery room birth." After our baby was born, they asked me what my occupation was in order to prepare the paperwork. They expected me to say "housewife." I answered, "Domestic Engineer." My independent and decidedly feminist ways passed down to the next generation as is evident on my daughter's birth certificate.

I was elated when Dennis finished his work in south Texas. We were once again headed back to California. I packed as much as I could before I flew home with both kids. Dennis planned to drive the rental truck across country. I realized later that I was so eager to leave Texas I left the entire kitchen for him to pack by himself. I am sure he was less than happy with me at that point. I think he was just as ready to move, because he dumped all the contents from the drawers and cupboards into one giant clothing box. I didn't care. Like Dorothy, I had clicked my ruby slippers three times and was finally going home.

7

Girl Scout Leader, Part Time Teacher, Faculty Wife – Oh My!

We arrived in California with hope for a good life and excited to find a new home. We bought a sweet little house and enjoyed Christmas holidays, birthday parties, and Easter egg hunts. There was much offered in this university town and we took advantage of all of it.

William and Louise participated in Scouts, soccer, and Little League baseball. Dennis spent many Saturdays keeping score at William's games or driving Louise to her soccer tournaments. I attended some of the games, but apparently embarrassed William. The bases were loaded and it was the top of the ninth inning. William was up to bat. I yelled, "Hit it over the fence!" That is exactly what he did! Dennis jumped out of his seat, spilling the scorekeeper's paperwork all over the ground. It was after that game that William asked me not to come to any more of his games. I tried to honor his request, while at the same time encouraging him to continue to play baseball or do whatever he was most interested in. Our lives were busy and the years sped by.

There were unspoken rules about a "way of being" in this small university town. Louise, at the age of five said, "I don't want to play soccer because all the parents are mean and yell at their kids." I told her she did not have to play. Most parents in the town considered not putting my child on a soccer team when she was five years old to be an extremely radical decision. After all, anyone who was anyone enrolled their kid in soccer by the time they were five or six. In my mind, that was reason enough to encourage Louise to play only if she wanted to and only if she felt safe around the other parents. Once she was a bit older, her friends encouraged her to play and she thoroughly enjoyed it.

William and Louise learned much about teamwork and competition as they grew up, which I believe formed them for their college experiences and ultimately their careers. They also learned early in life not to adhere to "shoulds" or to placate for the sake of fitting in or being accepted. I like to think we had some influence in those lessons. Our children undoubtedly learned more from the mistakes we made than from our futile efforts to be perfect parents.

I admit I was not the best professor's wife. For whatever reason, I never seemed to fit in the upper class and many professors and university-affiliated people acted as if they were better than anyone else was. The need to have their, as I call them, "certified smart letters," acknowledged after their name often grated on me. I am well aware it takes hard work to get a PhD. Once achieved it is not worth a dime if it is only used to look down on someone who has not had the same opportunities. It is not right to take one's fortune or success and turn it into a whip to beat others down. My parents taught me to take what you achieve or acquire in life and use it to help those who may be less fortunate.

I am passionate about social justice and I wrote more than

one letter to the editor of the local newspaper. My comments were not always positive, especially if it involved the police or any discrimination or bias toward women. One rather terse letter I wrote completely embarrassed Dennis, who was well on his way to becoming a full professor. He criticized me later on how wrong I was to write it, especially when our last name was printed for all to see.

At any rate, I was not going to stand idly by while police attempted to arrest a mother during a traffic violation. They followed her into the parking lot of the school while the children were outside at recess. In the middle of being questioned by the police, she bolted after her two-year-old who was about to run out into busy traffic. Then in one swift move, the police handcuffed her for attempting to evade the police. I was standing just six feet away watching in shock as the whole event unfolded.

The children at the picnic tables were horrified to see the mother of one of their friends handcuffed by a police officer. At that young age, they believed the police were supposed to help you, and this was not helping! I suppose my letter was more of a scolding of the police officer who (in my opinion) acted inappropriately. The mother and I became friends after that. I wondered if the police pulled her over because she was obviously by her dress, a foreigner. Once we became friends, she told me she was from Egypt and currently living in the United States. Discrimination, injustice, abuse, and lies do not sit well with me.

That was not the only time I embarrassed Dennis. I am sure there were several times over the years that he cringed when I spoke the truth. We once traveled to Hawaii. We enjoyed the islands and participated in some of the standard tourist attractions. We stopped at a booth where tourists could open an oyster for a chance to win a real pearl. The more you paid, the higher the chances were to win the prized pearl. I waited while

Dennis paid the money to the merchant. As I suspected, it was a scam. I became very upset when I saw the woman behind the booth switch the pearls while Dennis was paying the man in the front of the booth. I could not restrain myself and tried to tell the truth about what was happening. Dennis was very upset and accused me of ruining our trip. He said I should just be quiet and let the kids have fun.

On one level, I could agree with him. In reality, our children were deceived. My seething anger boiled over like hot lava from the volcano on the Big Island. I was determined to protect my children from deception and lies. As we flew home from Hawaii, I knew I overreacted to the switched pearl incident but I didn't have a clue what was beneath the surface of my strong reaction. I began to wonder about other times I may have overreacted in my life.

8

Tornado Swirling

After we returned home, I prayed about the numerous times I overreacted to a variety of events in my life. First, there was my unexplained dislike for having my picture taken. It was also obvious that I did not like to follow arbitrary rules or trust authority figures. I was often quick to judge the police. I hated playing games of any kind. My family learned that if they played a board game or other type of game, I watched them play or I read a book in the other room.

It seemed odd to me that people around me didn't have the same negative visceral reaction to cameras, games, or authority figures. Dennis made a comment one day when we were having an argument over yet another perceived injustice. He stopped mid-sentence and said, "Okay, I deserve about five percent of the anger you are spewing right now. But the other ninety-five percent belongs somewhere else." That dagger of truth stopped me cold. I knew he was right.

There were other indications that something was off. I was having severe, almost debilitating, headaches. We took a road trip to Canada, and Dennis pointed out that I consumed a large bottle of Tylenol in just two days. I couldn't get rid of the headaches. After we came home from that trip, my dentist determined I was grinding my teeth and clenching my jaw.

My temporal mandibular joint (TMJ) was the source of my headaches. A prescribed mouth guard helped relieve some of the pain. The dentist also suggested I see a therapist for stress relief and relaxation exercises.

I was a busy working mom. My teaching position took a great deal of energy as did the many social and sports activities the kids were involved in. I didn't have much time for therapy or relaxation exercises. However, I followed his recommendation and made an appointment with a therapist. The therapist seemed nice enough when we met, and she proceeded with the usual introductions and questions. I told her what the dentist said and only wanted her suggestions about how to relax and make my headaches go away.

The therapist asked about my history and family dynamics and I unemotionally responded. "My sister and I were five and three years old when my mother took us away from our father, and we lived somewhere with her and another man who was a cop. Then we ran away from him on the train because he was a bad guy. Then we ended up living in a hotel while our mom worked as a waitress in the restaurant on the ground floor. Something happened to our mother while we were locked in a closet, and she didn't come back to let us out. Somehow, Gayle and I ended up in foster care. We were adopted after we went through several foster homes. I grew up, got married, and now I have two kids. I found my birth father a while ago, and we are starting to talk on the phone. On our family vacation, I kept getting headaches and the dentist told me to see a therapist for relaxation exercises. Oh, and can you tell me how long this will take because I don't have a lot of money and I don't have a lot of time either."

The therapist slowly removed her glasses and placed them carefully in her lap. She sat there for a long time before she very quietly replied, "How about I drop my hourly fee twenty dollars and you come back and see me next week?" Little did I know those hours would turn into weeks and the weeks would turn into months. The woman with the steel blue eyes sitting across from me would become my very own Glinda… the good witch in the *Wizard of Oz*.

Very often tornados create a mess. The dark, twisted debris of my early childhood was untangled as I continued to meet with my therapist. One of the greatest gifts Dennis gave me, besides my children, of course, was helping me pay for therapy. If I did not have the opportunity to grieve my pain and understand why my life was in upheaval, I am not sure I would be here today. I am grateful for the marriage that Dennis and I had. I am also grateful for the tough lessons we both learned along the way. I grieved for many years over the pain we both suffered in the aftermath of that life tornado. Yet, God promises in Jeremiah 31:13, "I will turn their mourning into gladness; I will give them comfort and joy instead of sorrow."

I believe we each have a life-theme scripture verse. My life theme verse is Romans 8:28, "And we know that in all things God works for the good of those who love him, who have been called according to his purpose."

God worked our relationship and marriage for the good. Regardless of how things turned out, we each became the people we were meant to be. Dennis had a calm life with a secure upbringing and could not relate to what I experienced as a child, or with what we would face during our almost thirty years as a couple. In spite of the bumps and bruises in our marriage, we are friends now. I have no hard feelings toward Dennis. He is a wonderful father and grandfather.

We were so young when we met in 1970, and neither of us had seriously dated anyone else before we got married. Sadly, our marriage was ripped apart by that tornado.

9

The Heart of the Tinman

I could see the reason my therapist reduced her fee and asked me to return the following week. I didn't even flinch as I listed the facts of my childhood. In other words, I didn't feel a thing. The only indication that some emotion was there, was the small amount of feeling I allowed myself to express at locating my birth father. My therapist knew I repressed or otherwise stuffed and ignored the memories of my childhood traumas.

She was patient and careful. The wisdom of her years as a counselor told her she was sitting next to dynamite and even a small spark could blow away any hope of me continuing this "therapy thing" as I called it. We began with what I was feeling and that was my excitement at finally reuniting with my birth father.

When Louise was seven years old, she told me a story about something she did when she was five. It dawned on me later, as I was tucking her into bed, that my life at that age was a blank slate. I wondered how she could remember an event when she was five years old, yet I could not remember anything from that time in my life. I was curious and wanted to know more about my history. I also wanted my children to know about their DNA.

Our adoptive parents were smart people. They knew that eventually Gayle and I might want to know more about our family of origin. We were old enough to remember the woman visitor in the courthouse park and the man I called "the watch man," so my adoptive mother was not surprised when I told her I wanted to find my birth parents.

It was important that my adoptive mother knew just how much I loved her and appreciated her courage and strength. Our initial conversation was not easy for either of us, but she was supportive. She said, "You girls came to us when you were seven and nine years old. We have loved you and raised you since then, but you had a life before that. You have a right to your history. It is part of you. We always knew at least one of you would take this journey." I liked that word, journey. It was more than a search. I was not just searching for my birth parents or the answers to my vacant memories. I was on a journey to find...me.

I began my journey on January 10, 1989. My first thought was to find my birth mother. Somewhere in my mind I heard a voice saying ever so faintly, "Daddy's bad...Daddy's bad." I was apprehensive about what I would find. I heard stories of individuals who searched and, in the end...found only pain.

Regardless, I became obsessed with this new project in my life. I turned myself into a detective of sorts and used all available resources, including the Department of Motor Vehicles, the State Library, and telephone books. I had the photos the "watch man" gave to our adoptive parents. Gayle and I were toddlers in some of the photos, and there were photos of our birth parents too. Other than the photographs, I had little else to go on until our adoptive mother handed me a file of paperwork. My birth parent reunification search, or journey as I called it, changed my life in more ways than I can express.

I wanted as much information about birth parent reunification as I could find. It started with me asking my adoptive Mom lots of questions. She filled in some of the holes of the story of our adoption and our birth father signing the legal papers. She told me that it broke his heart, but he knew he needed to do what was best for both Gayle and me. He was grateful to our adoptive parents for giving us a stable home. When he came up to visit, he told them he did not have the room or the resources to care for us, too. Ultimately, he decided we would be better off with them.

He told them he was a "dry alcoholic" and still struggled with the addiction. He worked as a machinist and often worked the night shift. He came home late one night to find an empty house. My mother, Gayle, and I were gone. All he found was a note from our mother that she was leaving him and taking us with her. Our sudden disappearance tore him apart, and he drank himself into a stupor, drove off the road, and was in a nasty car accident. That is when he met his future wife. She was a nurse in the hospital where he was recovering. They married and adopted two girls. I wondered after I heard that, if he was trying to replace his stolen daughters.

The news that our father was heartbroken at our disappearance helped me see our adoption in a new light. It was not that my birth parents did not want me…or that I was so awful I caused them to go away. The truth was, the watch man, the man we used to call "daddy," the man who stood quietly in front of Gayle as she stretched out her arm to protect me… sacrificed so much when he signed those adoption papers. He sacrificed his heart. Our birth mother was too deep into her own addiction and personal challenges to take care of two small children. Her dysfunction is primarily what landed us in foster care.

I became obsessed with my birth parent search. I was a crazed woman on a mission. Nothing was going to stand in my way of finding the answers. Questions came up in my search for my mother. Of course, I was curious. Yet I could not explain the distance I felt. I wanted to know about her, but I felt nothing for her. I felt emotionally removed from her. When I thought about finding my father however, I felt loss, pain, and a deep need for comfort and love. Why was there a difference? My heart was searching for my father.

I attempted to find my mother, but something kept me from looking for her as diligently as I had for my father. I threw myself into research about birth parent reunification and read story after story of success and failure of others who tried to find their birth parents. I read about the legal aspects, the challenges, and the Pandora's Box that could open if in fact I found my birth parents. Some of the people who found their birth parents sadly discovered they were not interested in reuniting. I was discouraged until I picked up the last book in the stack on my desk. As I lifted the book, a small folded piece of paper fell out. It was a note written in scrawled handwriting. *If you are an adopted person and are reading this book to understand adoption more—please know that your birth parents have never forgotten you.* Signed, "A Birth Father." I sank to the floor and sobbed like a three-year-old.

This journey was taking a toll on my health, my job, and my family, and I needed a break. I was not sleeping or eating and was barely aware of my surroundings. I was frantic. My mind would not stop racing. I never imagined what an affect this search would have on me. I knew it was more than a search. As my adoptive mother said, it was a journey. Hal Aigner's book *Faint Trails* describes what many adopted children experience when they begin their searches: "For individuals, connection with a mystery classically occurs through means that are nonverbal and intuitive. Some would even go so far as to say that the process is spiritual. Such contact has a way of supplying answers to fundamental questions by virtue of making everything suddenly feel right. From that emotional state, a mystery can quickly transform into a bountiful source of inner satisfaction. But it can also be very demanding. It can insist that one make peace with it…before peace can be found anywhere else." [4]

That was what I was trying to do. I was trying to solve the mystery of my childhood. Why did our mother take Gayle and me away from our father? What happened to the happy family in the photos? Why couldn't I remember my early years? I was not just searching for answers. I was searching for peace. I knew if I gave up, I would never find that peace. Even though I knew I needed to rest from this journey, I was compelled to continue.

I researched the death index at the state library and didn't find my father's name. There was still hope he was alive. The DMV would have a record if he lived in California. What if he had moved out of state? How many state death indexes would I need to review to see if he was still living? It was overwhelming.

So much happened to us between the time our mother took us away from our daddy and our adoption. My mind flashed back once again to the day our birth father came to our front door. Gayle stood in front of me like a protective lion. She stared coldly at him and held her arm out in front of me as if to say, "Don't even try to touch her." I blinked out at him from behind her and thought to myself, *I know this man.* Reading the note in the book about adoption signed by a birth father fueled my determination. Although I was emotionally and physically exhausted, I made plans to go to the DMV the next day.

10

Joseph's Daughter

*M*y heart pounded as I walked into the DMV office. I whispered to myself, "Slow deep breath…Breathe." What would I say when they asked me why I wanted the record? My hand trembled as I clutched the wrinkled paper with my father's name and birth date. I managed to complete the form and nervously glanced over the information I wrote at the bottom of the page. Reason for search? "Organizing a family reunion." My conscience was trying to convince me I *was* organizing a family reunion…sort of. The person I was searching for would receive a copy of my request form so I was glad I rented a P.O. Box. I was protecting myself. I learned that lesson very early in life. Stay one step ahead…stay vigilant… always protect yourself.

After a never-ending wait, it was finally my turn at the window. The clerk barely looked at me when I handed him the request form with my father's information. Name, birth date, last known location. I also gave him my birth mother's name. I wondered if he could provide more information such as an address.

I needed to hold on to something as I waited for the clerk. My palms began to sweat as I tightly clenched the countertop. I swiftly wiped the counter with my arm to remove the perspiration and took another deep breath. "Stay calm…don't draw attention to yourself…don't be nervous…Breathe!"

"There is no record of this woman. But I do have information on the man." The clerk handed me the printed form, looked past me, and yelled out, "Next!"

I was shocked. I stumbled to the door as the next person in line stepped up to the window.

I pushed hard against the door as I left there, still grasping the paper in my hand. The icy January wind hit me full force. I could barely see through my tears, but there it was…my father's name and address! The birth date matched the information my adoptive mother gave me. He was still in Southern California. I found my birth father! Now I had even more questions. Will he want to talk to me? What will his family think? There was only one way to find out. I needed to contact him.

The wind tugged at me as I stumbled to my car. I drove in a daze to Dennis' office on campus. I needed someone to help me collect my thoughts and feel more centered before I took the next step on my journey. I arrived at Dennis' office and stood in his doorway, white with apprehension and still shaking. I handed him the paper and repeatedly said, "I can't believe it" as I slid into the chair next to his desk. There was no phone number on the paper. Dennis was already dialing Information Services in Southern California. My search for my father was about to be completed. The search for myself was just beginning.

_11_

There's No Place Like Home

$\mathcal{T}$he voice on the other end of the line was not that of an older man. This man sounded young. I held my breath, "May I speak to Joseph please?"

The young man responded with curiosity, "This is Joseph."

I pulled myself out of my stunned silence to explain that I was adopted and looking for my birth father. Now he was speechless. After a long pause, he said, "This is Joe Jr. Joseph is my dad."

I had no idea I had a younger brother! This news was almost too much to take in. I was not sure I heard what he asked. He repeated his question. "Which one are you?" He was asking if I was the one with blond hair or the one with brown hair. My birth father apparently mentioned us because Joe knew I had a sister. I said, "I am the blond one."

He seemed both hesitant and excited at the same time. I assume he knew what I was going to ask next. I asked if my father was still alive and if he might be willing to speak to me. He said he was indeed alive but had some health challenges. The bottom line was that my sudden appearance would definitely cause some concern for the rest of the family. My half-brother, though, was more than willing to pass along my information and ask his dad if I could speak to him.

Joe explained that his dad struggled with addiction and everyone in the family walked on eggshells. Most likely, he knew this sort of news could throw his father into an alcoholic tailspin. This was not going to be easy. His family was concerned about their dad keeping his sobriety. Before I could say more, Joe said he would call his father and then call me right back. I stood like a statue by the phone. Was this really happening? Was I actually going to speak to my birth father? What would happen if he said he did not want to hear from me? I read many stories of birth parent reunifications that did not end well. I was not prepared for a "no" if my newly found half-brother called me back and said it would be better if I didn't call.

The ring of the phone startled me out of my numbness. I drifted off into so many "what ifs," I didn't realize how long I stood there. Joe was on the other end of the line and said with excitement, "My dad said it would be fine if you called him… and here is his phone number."

In that moment, I could breathe deeply for the first time in over thirty years. My father was alive and he agreed to talk to me. The relief I felt when I heard my father was just a telephone call away was unbelievable! The daddy I lost more than thirty years ago, the man I thought of whenever I heard the Elvis Presley song "Love Me Tender." This man…the man who had a son…a son related to me…was within my reach.

I dialed the phone and only got halfway through the number before I hung up. My mouth was dry and my heart pounded. I dialed again. It rang a few times before a woman answered. I took a deep breath and asked to speak to Joseph. She wanted to know if I wanted Joe Jr. or Joe Sr. By now, the image of a lonely man in a rest home dissolved completely. The woman waited as I managed to whisper, "Joseph Sr. please."

Suddenly, a deep voice, raspy from years of smoking, said, "Hell-o?" I recognized that voice. I had heard it before. I was floating back in time. Faint verses of the Elvis Presley song my father sang to me as a lullaby echoed in my mind.

I cannot recall exactly what I said, but I think our conversation started with, "Joseph, my name is Cynthia. I don't want to upset you…but I am your daughter."

He was trying to grasp what was happening. His voice was even lower as he asked me in disbelief, "Cynthia?"

"Yes." I told him my birth date and that my mother's name was Betty.

He cleared his throat and said shakily, "Let's see here, I need to ask you some questions. Where were we living?"

I told him I didn't remember where we were living when I was with him, but I explained I was living with some foster parents and that he came to visit us just before we were adopted. I knew he would probably question my identity. He continued with more questions about my background and finally my answers satisfied him. His voice was shaky as he swallowed hard and said in barely a whisper, "That was so many years ago." I agreed and told him I would be thirty-five years old soon.

The rest of our conversation was a blur of questions I needed the answers to. His wife must have realized what was happening by then. I heard her telling him to get my address and phone number. I told him I wasn't sure about giving him my address but something made me trust him anyway. He asked if I ever had the opportunity to be in the area and all I could say was, "Possibly." He wanted to know how Gayle was and if she was happy. I assured him that she was and he seemed genuinely relieved.

Then he sounded stronger, more determined. He told me he thought I might be trying to find my mother and that he couldn't really help me with that. The last time he saw her was when he came up to visit us. He couldn't be sure, but he thought she was using drugs. He had no proof other than the fact that her arms were bruised and red. Then, before I knew it, I blurted out the question, "Is it true that Gayle was another man's child?" He hesitated briefly. "Yes, your mother was pregnant with Gayle when I met her. I adopted her as my own, but you were my daughter."

The impact of those words caught us both off guard. He choked back his tears as he explained that we left in the middle of the night and our mother took the car to the airport. She called him the next day and told him where the car was. She was also spending money faster than he could make it. He never thought she would just disappear with us in the middle of the night. I could hear the anger and desperation in his voice. My heart ached for the pain this man had endured. I wondered what I had done by calling him. As usual, I was blaming myself for someone else's pain. Somehow, it was my fault. Was this going to be too much for him?

He mentioned that he drove up to visit us before we were adopted and said it was obvious that if he wanted to say anything to me or get close to me...he would have to go through Gayle first. He was crying as he described our visit and said he knew we were terribly hurt. He seemed to have as many questions as I had and asked more about how I was able to locate him. He kept saying how pleased he was that I called and made the effort to find him. I thanked him for his time and said I hoped I hadn't upset him too much. He assured me that he was pleased to hear from me. He told me he would call or write. Then he said the words I desperately needed to hear. "I love you honey."

Through my tears I whispered, "I love you, too, Daddy." The dial tone echoed as I hugged the phone. January 18, 1989, I found my father. My heart had finally come home.

12

Lost and Found

The letter arrived on February 9. I knew it was from my father. I could have been blindfolded and known it was a letter from the man I was now referring to as "Dad." I inhaled deeply. Marlboro cigarettes. The smell of that brand of cigarettes meant safety and love. To this day, I can tell you which person in a crowded room smokes Marlboro cigarettes. It seemed a strange kind of thing to notice as I was growing up. Whenever someone walked by me on the street and they smelled like Marlboros, I stopped and stared to check their identity.

He printed the letter neatly and carefully, although there were some spelling errors. He also included the directions to his home. We planned to leave the kids with Dennis' mother and drive down to Southern California to meet my father. Dad was concerned about the recent snow on the Grapevine. Nothing would keep me from getting to my father now, not even a blizzard. I was desperate to be near him. I heard his voice. I wanted to feel the love and safety. Yet there was an underlying sense of anxiety, too.

We stayed one night with my adoptive mom on the way to Southern California. She knew I was nervous about the visit with my birth father. She told me he called her that afternoon to tell her how grateful he was for all the years they spent rais-

ing Gayle and me. Dad was concerned about the snow and
wanted me to call him before I traveled over the Grapevine.
I smiled as I thought about the care that he was beginning to
show for me.

That night, we stayed in my old bedroom. I looked at the
familiar light fixture and pictures on the walls, thinking about
what would happen the next day. What if he changed his mind
and decided not to see me at the last minute? Fear of rejection
was a part of my life. Once again, I was trying to protect myself from hoping for the good. I had a habit of seeing only the
bad that might happen in a situation. I taught myself never to
expect good in my life. That way, I wouldn't feel the pain and
disappointment when my hopes were dashed.

The weather was beautiful on the way to Los Angeles. The
sun was shining as we drove over the Grapevine. The snow
from the recent storm melted into tiny waterfalls along the
side of the road. We came to the top of a steep hill and I said,
"Right here!"

Dennis took his attention off the car in front of him. "What
did you say?"

"Right here!" I pointed to the wide fields of snow-covered
ground along the freeway. "This is where the snow pictures in
my photo album were taken. I know this place!"

He glanced to where I was pointing as he passed the slower
cars in the right lane and started to tell me those pictures could
have been taken anywhere, but he stopped mid-sentence. "I
guess you would know." We rode in silence until we reached
the valley below.

We stopped for lunch and went to a flower shop to pick up
a gift for my father and his wife, Madge. His wife was most
likely apprehensive about our arrival. I guess I was trying to
soften the blow. I wanted to show my appreciation for putting
up with my visit. I saw myself as an intruder in their lives and

always felt like I was in someone's way. In spite of all I had accomplished in life, I felt like I didn't belong. I didn't just apologize for my mistakes. I believed I was a mistake.

No cards were appropriate for an occasion like this. No one was celebrating a birthday. No one had started a new job or was graduating. I was stalling. Dennis knew it too. He reminded me I wouldn't find a card for this occasion. He was right. What kind of card would I find? One that said, "Hi, I'm back, it's been a long time." Or maybe a card that said, "Did you miss me?" I *was* stalling! It had been almost as many years since the man I was about to meet sat in a courtroom and willingly signed the consent for adoption form. Tears stung my eyes as I paid for the houseplant and blank card in my hand.

I held my breath as we drove the few short blocks to my father's house. Dennis kept repeating, "You can do this…you can do this!" At the time, he appeared to be a tower of strength. The truth is he was just as nervous as I was. Neither of us knew what we were getting into. He pulled the car to a stop in front of their house.

I turned to look at the man across the street. There he was! He was older than he was in the photographs, of course. I don't know what I expected. Maybe I thought he would look the same as he did in the thirty-year-old photos tucked carefully in my suitcase. The picture I was looking at wasn't in a photo album. This was an old man walking deliberately toward the car. I couldn't move. Finally, I released the seatbelt and grasped the door handle as I cautiously stepped out of the car.

I resembled the man directly in front of me. Louise looked like him too. I saw where she got her wide-set brown eyes and where William got his receding hairline. This man, this nearly bald old man…was Louise and William's grandfather and my father!

My father took me in his arms and hugged me. He held me like a fragile china doll. I inhaled a mixture of familiar men's cologne and Marlboro cigarettes. Surprisingly, there were no tears for either of us when we first hugged. He said it had been a long time and asked how I was doing. "I'm hanging in there." He took my hand in his as we walked up the steps to his front door, brushed away a tear and cleared his throat, "Me too honey…me too."

His wife opened the door and greeted us. She was straightening up and seemed apprehensive and annoyed at the same time. Although she attempted to be gracious, I sensed her irritation. I can't say I blame her. The whole experience was a shock to all of us. The initial introductions were awkward. We chatted briefly about the weather, the snow on the Grapevine, and our drive down. My dad made me a cup of coffee and added just the right amount of cream and sugar. It was exactly how I would have made it.

It wasn't long before my father told the same story he told me on the phone. He talked about my mother spending more money than he could make and about the visit to our adoptive parent's home. He said he tried to find us but hadn't been able to. He also told us about his alcoholism and that he had not had a drink in two years. His voice started to crack. I knew his life had been difficult. My sudden reappearance was bringing up old pain he tried to drown in alcohol.

We hadn't talked long when Joe walked in. My dad introduced us to his son. He was a builder by trade and played the bass guitar. I was pleasantly surprised. William was learning how to play the bass, too. Joe was polite, clean-cut, and shy. He seemed genuinely interested in meeting us. I detected his curiosity on the phone when we talked for the first time in January. He didn't have any siblings related to him. My father and his wife adopted both of Joe's sisters when they were babies. He had a family relationship with them, but no hereditary link. I was his half-sister. I shared his DNA.

Dad commented how much we looked like each other. Joe was taller, younger, and blond like me. There were similarities and anyone could tell we were related if they saw us together. The first sign of Madge's animosity flared as she said sharply. "Joe looks like my father!" She wasn't going to admit any resemblance between us. It was evident this woman wasn't ready to accept me.

My dad insisted that Joe and I stand together so he could take our picture. Then Dennis took pictures of all three of us together. The pictures and cameras reminded Dennis about my childhood photo album in the car. I brought my wedding album, too, because I thought my father would want to be part of his daughter's wedding day in one way or another. Weddings were on their minds because Joe was getting married in June.

I watched my father carefully as he slowly turned the pages of the photo album he had given our adoptive parents. Madge was watching too. She had been with this man for thirty years and could read him like a book.

It was Dad's turn to travel back in time now. He saw his child in those pictures. The baby...the toddler...the three-year-old ripped from his life. A sadness washed over him as he looked at photos of my mother. He always loved her. He looked at me as if to acknowledge her features. He looked again at the photos of Gayle in the park and whispered, "She has her mother's hair."

Joe looked at the album over his father's shoulder, and they both stopped at the snow pictures. "Do you know where those pictures were taken of you and Gayle?" Dennis and I glanced at each other as we waited for the answer. "Frazier Park off of the Grapevine." I pointed out that exact place on our way over the mountains. I knew it! I felt like I was recovering from amnesia. Memories of people and places were beginning to come back to me. Then an eerie sensation floated through the room. Maybe Madge stiffened or clenched her jaw and my father could feel it. He closed the album and got up to get me another cup of coffee. I thanked him and said I was fine. The truth is I was already shaky enough. He lit his cigarette and I inhaled the scent of Marlboros and felt safe once again.

The visit became more frenetic as more people dropped in. I wondered if they told the whole county we were visiting. I wasn't comfortable on display like that. I never liked being the center of attention in any crowd. My privacy was important to me and I felt like a freak in a circus show. First, some of Joe's friends stopped by and then his fiancé. His fiancé was warm and friendly and sat down to chat about their wedding. She was very interested in our wedding album. She flipped through the pictures and innocently commented about how floral dresses were back in style for weddings. Joe was eleven years younger than I was. Dennis grinned teasingly at me as if to say, "You old bag." The conversation and connecting bonds were healing deep places of loss that no words could express.

The afternoon passed as we chatted about the roses planted in their back yard and the wedding plans for Joe and Jen. We spent little time talking about my childhood. It was painful for all of us and I knew the topic was too sensitive. I said I was sorry it had taken me so long to contact him. Madge unexpectedly asked Dennis if he wanted to go outside to look at the roses. I suppose she was offering my father and me a few minutes alone together. I looked out the window as Dennis and Madge talked in the backyard. My father and I sat quietly at the kitchen table. Finally, he said tenderly, "I'm glad you contacted me."

I couldn't tell him what I wanted to say. I didn't know where to start. He wasn't sure what to say either. I told him again I was sorry I hadn't found him sooner. Just then, Madge and Dennis entered the room and she started barking orders. He jumped like a trained animal. What was that feeling? What did I hear? A cold angry voice inside of me growled, "She has castrated him!" I knew then what I was feeling. It was a distant anger. No, it was more of a rage at "the mother" for the way she was treating him. This was old stuff.

It was a long, stressful afternoon so we agreed to rest and meet again for dinner. Dad kissed me goodbye and said he would see us later. As we got in the car, Madge told us about their daughter who lived down the street and how Dad drove the grandchildren to school every day and how important their family was to them. I knew what she was saying. She didn't need to draw me a picture. They had a life and I wasn't a part of it. I was a visitor in their home…that was all.

My tears flowed as our car pulled away from the curb. The stress of the afternoon overwhelmed me. This was too hard. I wanted a glass of wine. No, at that moment, I needed a glass of wine.

13

Connecting

Madge allowed my father to sit near me as we ate dinner in a crowded Mexican restaurant. She sat at the opposite end of the table and loudly announced that she needed a drink. She scowled at me as if to say, "And of course we all know why I need a drink."

My nerves were shot and I longed for a glass of wine, but I ordered decaf instead. Dad ordered coffee, too. It was wonderful to be near him. I wanted to get as much as I could from him in the short time we had left together. We still had not talked much about my childhood. The crowded, noisy restaurant wasn't making it any easier. I asked him a few questions while we waited for our dinner.

"Did we have any birds when we were little? I remember birds. Cages and cages of parakeets."

"We didn't have parakeets. It must have been that other man who owned all the bird cages."

Gayle and I didn't remember much about the other man. Another puzzle piece of my life suddenly fell into place. I recalled the few times that Gayle and I talked about our childhood. I always referred to that other man as "the birdman." Dad suggested I might have been remembering the chicken farm. He and my birth mother kept several chickens for a while and tried to make money that way. But she hurt her back and they couldn't keep up with the work.

The noise in the restaurant forced me to lean closer to my father in order for him to hear me. "Do you remember the Elvis Presley song, 'Love Me Tender'?" I didn't tell him how important that song was to me. I just knew whenever I heard it I was overcome with a sense of sadness and loss of my daddy.

Dad sat quietly and nervously stared into his coffee cup, then mumbled, "No, I don't think I know that song." He didn't look at me when he answered and continued to stare into his cup. I didn't believe his answer. Our dinners were ready and that was the end to any more questions.

The conversation shifted to Joe's wedding and other topics. I didn't have any appetite and wasn't eating much. My eyes drifted to the bartender pouring a glass of wine for a customer.

"You're not eating much."

I kept my attention focused on my plate as I explained to my father that I was just tired. He understood. The tension of the last twelve hours was taking a toll on all of us. We got up to leave the restaurant and I helped him with his coat. I reached for the hat he had carefully placed under his chair and I gently touched his arm. It wasn't enough. I was close. I wanted to be closer.

After dinner, Madge drove us back to the motel as she explained that Dad didn't like to drive at night. He was silent as he rode in the front passenger seat. Madge and Dennis carried on a lively conversation, but I was too tired and weak to say anything at all. The car stopped and Dad jumped out of the front seat. Suddenly, he pulled me into his arms and held me close. This time, it was a strong, secure hug. "I do love you. You know that don't you?" He was determined to convince me of his love while at the same time fearful of what Madge would say or do next.

I held on tightly and whispered, "I hope my visit hasn't been too hard on you." He smiled and said it was fine. We agreed to stop by their house in the morning before we left town, then said good night. I was lost in my thoughts as Dennis and I slowly walked back to the motel room. I was certain I would have more answers about my childhood by now. Instead, my mind was spinning with more questions.

Exhausted, I climbed into bed and wrote in my journal. We planned an early breakfast with Joe and Jen at the coffee shop next to our motel, but I wanted to write some notes before I went to sleep. I reviewed all that Dad said. He told me our birth mother was a good mom. She just got into trouble with the drugs. My mind flashed to the expression on my father's face when I asked about the Elvis Presley song. A familiar sadness came over him then. That bothered me. But there was something else that was bothering me more. Why did I feel a desperation to hold on to him? I shook it off and convinced myself this reunification process would eventually smooth out.

Dennis was snoring as I wrote a list of everything I wanted my father to know, and then I wrote him a long letter. I told him how sorry I was for the hell my birth mother caused him. I also told him I did not intend to disrupt his current relationship and family. I ended my letter with "I love you." If Madge would not let me tell my father these things, I could at least put my thoughts and feelings in a letter and hand it directly to him in the morning. Emotionally and physically exhausted, I fell asleep with the pen in my hand.

14

Echoes from the Past

I didn't get much sleep in spite of the exhaustion I felt the night before. I woke up several times as I tossed and turned throughout the night. I was lost in my thoughts as I waited in the motel lobby. Dennis, Joe, and Jen were all standing in the parking lot trying to get my attention. It was strange how I could suddenly be in another world oblivious to what was happening around me. I hastily swallowed the last drop of my coffee and headed for the parking lot.

My half-brother and I definitely resembled each other. He had the same round face that schoolmates had teased me about when I was a child. His hair was blond and he had blue eyes. Jen was sweet yet also a "take charge" kind of gal. I think she was curious about me. After all, she would marry this man in a few short months and eventually be affected by our new and still awkward sibling relationship.

At breakfast, Joe and I talked about his job and how he met Jen and a little about his childhood. The smell of coffee, cigarettes, and syrup washed over me. I methodically buttered my toast and was suddenly in another time and place. I never liked coffee shops. It had always been difficult for me to eat breakfast in one.

"Would you like more coffee?"

I didn't see the server standing next to me until she spoke. I startled and realized I also missed part of the conversation Dennis was having with Joe. "I'll have decaf this time."

Joe ordered breakfast and I teased him about eating every bite on his plate. We laughed and teased each other as we joked back and forth. I knew this young man. I felt connected. He was gentle and caring and it all felt comfortable and familiar. Once more, my thoughts wandered to beaches and birthday cakes, lullabies and Elvis Presley songs.

It was embarrassing for me to drift off like that. It seemed to be happening more often lately. I shrugged it off as exhaustion and watched as my new brother finished his very large breakfast. I smiled as he talked about his business and his struggle with asking people to pay their bills on time. His gentle spirit was evident as he quietly changed the subject and for the first time, asked me questions about my childhood.

I shared what I knew about our birth mother leaving us locked alone in a hotel closet and the various foster homes Gayle and I lived in after the hotel manager found us.

His blue eyes softened, "That must have been very difficult." He was genuine. He was kind. I felt lucky to have found him. He added that knowing how important family was to his father, what happened to Gayle and me must have devastated his dad.

I agreed. "Your father and I were loved and hurt by the same woman." That was the only time in our conversation that my voice cracked.

Dennis sensed the need to move on. "Shall we go?"

I needed a moment to pull myself together so I headed for the restroom. I was tired and vulnerable, but I didn't want to fall apart. I had to hold it together in front of my half-brother. I looked in the mirror and applied makeup over the dark circles that were now obvious under my eyes. It was hopeless. I might as well admit this weekend…this visit…this small talk had taken a toll on me.

Dennis and Joe walked out to the car, but Jen waited in the hall for me as I came out of the restroom. She slipped her arm around my waist and said, "I really admire you for what you are doing."

I barely knew this young woman, but it was an affirmation for the decision to find my birth father. I thanked her as I returned her hug. There was a distinct shift in my posture and the more flippant part of my personality came out. I tossed my head back and laughed pointing at Joe, "I bet you didn't know what you were getting yourself into when you agreed to marry that guy." I shifted from feeling vulnerable to a toughness and strength of personality that had been with me for as long as I could remember.

The fresh air was a welcome relief as the door of the coffee shop closed behind me. No more coffee, no more syrup and cigarettes. I took a long, deep breath as we walked to the car and thought of my birth mother working in the coffee shop in the hotel. She was the reason I hated coffee shops. My comment to my half-brother at breakfast echoed, "Your father and I were loved and hurt by the same woman." I tallied the losses my father and I endured over the years. I wanted to make up for that. A voice in my head said, "I can do this." At the same time another voice whined, "I am tired…I want to go home now."

There was an odd mix of curiosity and anxiety as we headed toward an area of town where my father said we lived. Joe knew how to find some of the places his dad pointed out the day before. He looked at the photo album again to see if he recognized any of the locations. I considered asking my father to go with me and debated whether to invite him. He spent a lifetime trying to forget the pain and memories of our past life. I had dug up what he had buried long ago and decided it would have been too hard for both of us. Joe and Jen on the other hand, understood my need to visit my past and complete my journey.

Dennis drove as we crossed some railroad tracks and came to a much older neighborhood. The houses, built in the 1950s, were out in the hills a distance from town. They all noticed my silence, and I was certain they could hear my pounding heart as we rode without speaking. We came to an open area with large trees, old picnic tables, and a shed that looked like an old army barracks. The question caught in my throat. "What is this place?"

Joe offered, "It's a park."

Dennis glanced at me in the rearview mirror and slowed the car to a stop. We were still a distance from the park, but I was already out of the car and almost running toward the playground.

The slide...the merry-go-round...the swings! I desperately wanted to stay in control but I was already crying. Joe and Jen waited in awkward silence as I stood there shaking until Joe put his arm around me. My reaction to the park was more than any of us expected. Dennis hurried back to the car for the photo album and camera. I walked in a daze toward the merry-go-round and then the tree...the shed...the huge rocks at the edge of the park and back to the merry-go-round where I sat down, buried my face in my hands, and wept.

There were only four of us in the park that day. I felt more. The children...the people...so many people. What had I begun? What Pandora's Box had I opened now? My eyes blurred with tears as I asked Dennis to take a picture of the playground, the tree, the rocks, and the shed. I noticed the railroad track again. I didn't like railroad tracks and I didn't like losing control. I was angry that I felt vulnerable and completely drained of what little energy I had left.

We took the pictures we needed, and I mumbled an apology for my emotional breakdown as we headed back to the car. The tree stood solemnly in the middle of the park. I had a haunting feeling I had been there before. I told myself I was feeling the loss of happy times but there was something else. I couldn't explain the chill that ran through me as we left that park, and I collapsed in the back seat as we drove away in silence.

Dennis and I stopped by my father's house on our way out of town. I was relieved that our visit was almost over. When my father opened the door, I quickly handed him the letter I wrote the night before. He secretly tucked it into his pocket without looking at it. It was futile to think I could fully express my feelings about the loss of our relationship in just one letter. We were both emotionally exhausted. This reunion opened doors we weren't ready for. The memories never healed for my father. He tried to drown his pain with alcohol. I on the other hand, blocked the memories out of my mind completely. I always believed my life started when I was adopted. Didn't everyone have black holes in their childhood? Dad gave me a kiss good-bye. I hugged him and inhaled deeply. The scent of Marlboro cigarettes lingered in the car. Once again…my daddy was gone.

15

Tentative Beginnings and the Wicked Witch

My father called on the weekends to see how I was doing and I wrote him letters every week. I couldn't get enough of him. I was so desperate to hear his voice that Dennis worried about the compulsive nature of our new relationship.

I told my father I searched for my birth mother. He was careful in his warning on the phone.

"I don't want you to take this the wrong way but I don't think it's a good idea to pursue your mother. If you find her and she is still on that kick, she could just hurt you more." He said if I did find her, she could just lie about things. He never told me what he meant by "on that kick" or what she might lie about. He was careful in choosing his words in an effort to protect me. Then the tone of his voice became more serious and directive. He repeated his warning. "I don't think you should be looking for your mother. I am concerned she could just hurt you more." I sensed an internal confirmation of the truth of his advice and assured him I had no desire to find my mother. I only wanted to find him.

Our communication continued for several months and the man I was now calling "Dad" said little about my childhood other than eluding to the fact that finding my mother could cause trouble. Perhaps his wife was still jealous of his relationship with my birth mother. It wasn't difficult to notice when he looked at the photo album that he hadn't forgotten her. Yet, there was almost a pleading in his voice when he tried to persuade me not to look for her.

Dad called me whenever Madge was out of the house. She wasn't just jealous of my mother, she was also jealous of me. Whenever I called him, our conversations were guarded and brief, especially if she was home. My father was a different person when she was around. The sense that I was the sordid family secret became stronger, and my resentment toward Madge grew. Once again, "the mother" was keeping me from my father. My jaw tightened as I recognized a familiar anger.

Slowly the pain and need for comfort came out in my letters. He called and said he was concerned that bringing all these memories back up could make me sick. I told him it might be painful but it was for the best. It was time I dealt with my past.

Gayle had Dad's address, but she hadn't written to him. I guess she figured this relationship belonged to me. She found out we were not full sisters, and that was a blow to both of us, but she didn't admit her pain either. Dad suggested Gayle was trying to protect me and did not write to her because he didn't want to interfere. He wanted everything to work out where no one was hurt.

My journey of self-discovery was supposed to provide answers. Yet I kept coming up with more questions. I wanted Gayle to have a connection to her DNA. In spite of my father's warning, I decided I needed to find my mother if not for me, at least for Gayle.

I started a second search for my birth mother with little enthusiasm and much anxiety. We had different fathers but

Gayle and I shared our mother's DNA. As I told my birth father, I didn't have a need to find my mother as much as I wanted to find him. Honestly, I just wanted to avoid the whole process. Obligation plus my constant desire to please my sister propelled me forward.

Gayle took on the role of mother when we were very young. I always looked up to her and wanted to please her and do what she said. When Gayle told me to be quiet, I was quiet. When she criticized me or got angry with me, my world crashed. For my preschool and early years, she was the only family I had. Until I found my birth father, she was the only other person in the world who was my blood relative.

Once again, I went to the DMV to try to locate my birth mother. I had her information from my adoptive parent's records. This time I searched under an alias our birth mother used when she was arrested for stealing a car. Our adoptive parents kept a newspaper article about her arrest and her alias was in the article.

I stepped up to the counter still wearing my sunglasses.

"May I help you?"

I froze as the man took the form from my hand. It was the same clerk! Fortunately, he was more interested in entering the data into the computer than focusing on me. Suddenly he stopped what he was doing and asked, "Are you sure someone else isn't looking for this woman? This information seems very familiar."

I tried to calm myself to control the rising panic. I didn't want to blow this. My body went numb. I felt like an actor on stage with the direction to appear irritated and heard myself say, "Oh, I am so frustrated with this whole family reunion nonsense! We're trying to get together and I suppose if you can't find anything on her I will just have to give up and tell the rest of the family to do the search themselves!"

The clerk detected my well-acted irritation and innocently offered, "There is a Betty B. with this last name you've given, but her birthdate is not the same." Then he added, "It was common for women to lie about their age during that time period." He seemed pleased with himself for providing that helpful bit of information.

That was my cue. I flipped my hair back and said, "Oh really? That's fascinating! It could possibly be the woman I'm looking for." I flashed him a smile. "You have been very helpful."

The clerk happily handed me the form. I walked away staring at the paper and reviewed my research on our mother. It wasn't painting a pretty picture. I knew she was an alcoholic and drug addict and she took us away from our father in the middle of the night. She worked as a waitress at a sleazy coffee shop and frequently locked us in the hotel closet when she wanted to go to a bar or out with a man. She had stolen a car and used an alias. Great! At this point I was beginning to wonder if Jesse James would appear somewhere in our family tree.

Somehow, I knew exactly what to do to get what I needed. I didn't like what just happened, but I was desperate to do whatever it took to locate our mother for Gayle's sake. I had no desire to meet our mother or locate her for any other reason than to give Gayle the opportunity to find a birth parent. Maybe the paper I was holding would be the missing piece to the puzzle of our lives. The harsh voice in my head said, "If your mother was a con-artist, you may have inherited some tricks from the old gal."

The description on the paper was chillingly close to the pictures of our mother. Brown hair and green eyes. Gayle has brownish red hair and hazel-green eyes. The first name was correct and the middle initial she used was the same as her last name before she was married. Everything was the same except the birth date. Then I heard someone say, "Don't get your hopes up kid, they will only be dashed." I looked up to see who had spoken to me. There was no one there.

It had only been three days since my acting debut in the DMV when the phone rang.

"Is this Cynthia?"

"Yes."

The woman on the phone identified herself as a supervisor at the DMV. She asked if I had submitted search papers for a Betty B. I felt the familiar childhood panic of doom. I had done something wrong. It was my fault. Childhood pain flooded over me like the drenching nightmares I had after our mother locked us in the hotel closet. I ignored my dizziness and clenched my fists as I tried to focus on what the woman was saying.

The supervisor explained in a frustrated tone that since the data did not exactly match the dates and facts I provided, the clerk should not have given me the report. "My clerk was wrong to give you that information," she said harshly.

I apologized and told her the clerk suggested it might be accurate. What she said next nearly knocked me over. "The woman you were researching called my office this morning and says she doesn't know you. She is threatening to sue us!"

I didn't intend to cause a problem. "I think your clerk was just trying to be helpful. I didn't mean to cause any trouble." She understood my concern for her clerk but clearly repeated the point that I should not have been given the information. I felt like a small child and faintly heard the words, "I'm a bad girl…bad girl" running through my mind. It was wrong to get what I needed. It had always been wrong to get what I needed.

I frantically tried to fix the wrong I committed. "I would be happy to write to the woman and apologize if that would help."

"No!" she snapped. Then she stammered and abruptly ended our call with, "The woman says she doesn't know you and… and… doesn't want you to contact her!"

I knew the DMV would notify the woman I was researching. Yet it had only been three days! I was glad I used a P.O. Box number as my return address. My father's warnings about my mother echoed, "She could just hurt you more." The woman I found was obviously upset enough to threaten a lawsuit. It seemed to me if it were an innocent mistake of identity, the person contacted would simply inform the DMV of the error. It bothered me that she made a specific request that I not contact her. Why was the woman so upset? Whoever she was, she was scared. Could this woman actually be my birth mother? If so, she was once again on the run.

This time the shift in my body was more obvious. I no longer felt dread, panic, or guilt for the wrongs I committed. In fact, there was no feeling whatsoever as I heard a voice say with sly laughter, "Wouldn't it be something if the con-artist was out-conned by her own daughter?"

16

Cowardly Lion

I began to let go of (or let out rather) the frightening memories of what happened to me when I was five and younger. I was most likely able to do this because I felt "safe enough" after connecting with my birth father. My curiosity as to why Louise could remember what happened in her early years broke open my own Pandora's Box. The blank slate of my childhood filled up with scenes out of a horror movie.

The best way to describe what was happening to me is Post Traumatic Stress Disorder (PTSD). Much like a war veteran, little things would set off or trigger my traumatic memories. I was thirty-nine years old by the time these memories began to surface. I recall one particular time when a simple television commercial about a train threw me back to a frightening experience when I was quite small. The next thing I knew, I was curled up in a fetal position on the floor in the laundry room and desperately tried to catch my breath between my sobs. I felt completely out of control. I know I would not be here today if I tried to live through those horrific memories without God in my life.

My communication with my father over just a few weeks allowed me to piece together some of the more traumatic abuse Gayle and I endured with the stepfather, or the birdman as we called him. He was a sadistic pedophile and repeatedly abused us while our mother grew more dependent upon him for her drugs. My memories of the physical, sexual, and spiritual abuse came out in pictures or images, and I often drew them on paper in order to tell my story. That is just one way I found emotional release from the fear and torture we endured as children.

I want to make it clear that I did not have these memories in the therapist's office. Rather, the memories came out in dreams and at home, almost on a daily basis in those first few months. After that, I went to my therapist who helped me grieve and process the crushing pain of it all. I say this because at the time I was recovering these memories, there was a group calling themselves the False Memory Syndrome Foundation. This organization tried to convince therapists and the public that false memories of horrific physical, sexual, and spiritual abuse were planted in survivors by therapists. They were determined to negate the truth of many survivors of abuse. My ability to recover my own memories outside of the therapist's office helped me know that I wasn't making up what was surfacing from my childhood, and my therapist did not plant any false memories in me.

There was a reason this organization didn't want victims remembering abuse from their childhood. They tried to create doubt about the accuracy of the memories survivors had to protect their own personal interests. The claims of this organization have been questioned over time. In fact, one author stated, "In 1992, the parents of Jennifer Freyd, who had accused her father of sexual assault, founded the False Memory Syndrome Foundation. The parents maintained Jennifer's accusations were false and encouraged by recovered memory therapy. While the foundation has claimed false memories of abuse are easily created by therapies of dubious validity, there is no good evidence of a 'false memory syndrome' that can be reliably defined, or any evidence of how widespread the use of these types of therapies might be."[5]

Lies thrive in darkness and liars will use any method to prevent the truth from coming into the light. I knew at the core of my being that I wasn't making up what I was remembering. The fact is one cannot heal from a wound that is not there. I was healing, and God was with me every step of the way.

Unfortunately, I was initially confused about which daddy some of the memories were associated with and confronted my father on the phone. He was very gentle. He told me again that he knew Gayle and I suffered greatly and that we were hurt in many ways. It grieved his heart when he saw us in 1960. He allowed me to ask him specific questions and patiently answered them. By the end of the conversation, I was reassured that he was the "safe daddy" and not the daddy who hurt us.

The day after our conversation, I was flooded with more memories about the stepfather who was clearly the daddy who abused us. In fact during one of my PTSD episodes, I kept repeating the words, "*my* daddy wouldn't let this happen." The truth was clear. My daddy was my protector. Now it all made sense!

Everything I repressed or intentionally forgot came oozing to the surface when I found my birth father. It was safe to remember the painful trauma because my "protector" was in my life again. That also explained the compulsion to find him and my desperate need to feel the safety and comfort of my daddy's arms.

Much like the full picture on the front of a puzzle box, the pieces of my life began to fall into place. It was not my father who abused us…it was the stepfather. He was a pedophile and a cop who produced child pornography. That explained my aversion for having my picture taken and my life long distrust of the police. Two more puzzle pieces fell into place.

Shortly after this realization, my father and I talked on the phone about my confusion. I told him that I now understood he was my "safe daddy" and not the "bad daddy." At the end of that call as with every one of our previous conversations, he said, "I love you, honey." I thanked him for his understanding and patience and ended our call with, "I love you, too."

17

Ruby Slippers

I mentioned to my therapist that finding myself was similar to being Dorothy in the *Wizard of Oz*. I looked for happiness and peace by keeping busy, drinking alcohol, or over working. All the while, happiness was right there in my own back yard or put more directly, in my relationship with Jesus.

My father and I communicated for about six months. It was wonderful! I was putting my life together again through this reunification until my life shattered like glass when he called me one late August afternoon.

He stammered as he told me that contacting him caused some problems in his marriage and he was upset and wanted to drink again. He shared in previous conversations that his wife was jealous of our relationship. They had adopted two girls, and Madge was afraid that her adopted daughters would want to start searching for their birth parents.

I was in shock and couldn't breathe as I tried to take in what he was telling me.

"I think we need to break this off."

I couldn't believe what I was hearing. My heart pounded, my throat ached, and I felt dizzy and sick to my stomach. I was in a full-blown panic attack. I knew I asked too many questions. This didn't make sense! My questions in our conversation the day before had not upset him. He was loving and reassuring.

In that previous conversation, he said he knew Gayle and I lived in several child welfare homes and there were many different "daddies." He wasn't angry or upset when I asked him those searching questions. He wanted to help. Now this sudden turn around? Something was terribly wrong!

He continued, "You told me I abused you…that I hurt you."

What? Where was this coming from? "No, I did not say that! What are you talking about?"

He fired off the next bizarre accusation. "You said you were going to sue me and accuse me of sexual abuse."

I was in disbelief as tears streamed down my face. "No! I never said that! I told you it was the stepfather. I was just asking questions to learn what happened to us. I never accused you or threatened to sue you!"

He repeated, "I think we need break this off. Maybe we can just send Christmas cards."

I heard the cold click of the phone on the other end of the line and crumpled to the floor in a flood of tears. The afternoon and evening passed in a fog of depression. My mind went numb and I heard angry voices and a sorrowful moaning from somewhere deep inside. My mood was as dark as the clouds and I wanted to die. Suddenly, thunder boomed, a bolt of lightning flashed and our electricity went out. Again, I was rocking back and forth in the dark void of a hotel closet from long ago.

That night I replayed our phone conversation over again in my mind. I frantically tried to recall everything he said, as I searched for what caused him to change his mind. Something was off with that phone call. Then I knew! My father wasn't saying those things *to* me, he was saying them *for* me! I remembered the odd silence at the beginning of our conversation and felt a glimmer of hope. I thought it was strange that his voice sounded like he was in an echo chamber and initially dismissed it as poor phone connection. Then it suddenly dawned on me that there were *two* clicks at the end of that call. Someone was listening on a second phone line! Intuitively I knew what happened. My father set up that phone call to prove to Madge that her accusations and assumptions about me were wrong. He must have convinced her to listen on the second phone line to prove my intentions in reuniting with him were genuine. He wanted her to hear me say that I had no plans to accuse him in any way. Through that painful and shocking phone conversation, my father was still protecting me.

The next morning I was on my knees praying and pleading with God. Okay, I admit it. I was angry and I was yelling at God. I felt betrayed. How could God take my father away from me again after all these years and only six months after we were reunited?

"God," I screamed, "you said that in all things you work for the good of those who love you who have been called according to your purpose." I continued my rant. "If this is true, I want a sign and I want it right now." I slammed my fist into the couch as I spewed on, "That even this will work for the good!"

That very moment the game show *Jeopardy* was on the television in the next room. It seemed as if the volume suddenly got louder because I clearly heard the host ask, "What character wore the ruby slippers?" The answer was, "Dorothy from the *Wizard of Oz*."

It wasn't much, but it was enough of a sign for me to hold on to hope. My awe and wonder at this tiny miracle…this possible answer from God, helped me get up off my knees and take another shaky step toward God's light at the end of what was now a long, dark tunnel.

18

A Thread of Hope

*G*od is still there when life gets tough. Some people may try to tell you that believing in God is just magical thinking. They may also tell you there is no God and that you have to do life all on your own. Here is the truth. You just can't "do life" all by yourself, at least not very well.

My personal faith is in Jesus Christ. More than once, I have argued with God about the way things happened in my life. God did not abandon me. Even when I screamed and slammed my fist into the couch. Some church leaders teach that it is not okay to be upset with God. They teach that as Christians, we should only say nice flowery things to God. Not true. Our God is bigger than our anger. God can take it. Expressing honest emotions leads to honest relationships, especially with God. One of my favorite scriptures is from Psalm 27:10. The Amplified Bible says it this way:

Although my father and my mother have abandoned me,
Yet the Lord will take me up (adopt me as His child.)

It took losing my birth father a second time before I embraced the truth of those words. Through the loss of my earthly father, I became more intimate with my heavenly Father. I was and will continue to be fully loved, fully forgiven, and fully accepted as a child of God. When I am angry or hurt and even shake my fist at God…He still loves and accepts me. I've learned that the love of Jesus can get me through anything life throws my way. Whenever I feel hopeless or feel as though the ground beneath me is crumbling, God will give me the wisdom, strength, and grace to stand strong.

After my father called and broke off our relationship, I didn't care about living any longer. Then I looked at my children and knew I could not abandon them as I had been abandoned. Although I didn't realize it at the time, God was preparing me to use the compassion born from my pain to help others who felt hopeless and discouraged.

God works in mysterious ways. I was depressed and suicidal and called the Suicide Hotline. When I called, I got a busy signal. Wait a minute! A busy signal? That wasn't supposed to happen. I called again…still a busy signal and then, the hotline hung up on me!

God knew me from before I was born. He knew I had a passion for righting the wrongs of injustice. The irony is I was bound and determined to stay alive long enough to call that hotline back and give them a piece of my mind. How dare they have the audacity to hang up on me in my time of distress! God tapped into my anger energy and that boost of energy is just one reason I am alive today. God turned a thin thread of hope into a mighty chain to pull me out of my abyss.

As time went on, my faith in God grew stronger. I surrounded myself with strong Christian friends and attended various support groups. My therapy continued and I immersed myself in the Word of God. It was a long road, but I'm very glad I persevered. The random puzzle pieces of my life fell together and created a clearer picture of who I was meant to be. In fact, I look at my daughter and admire her determination and perseverance. I believe that if I had not been abandoned and abused, I may have been just as strong and courageous as she is. I see the care and compassion of God in my son, and I am extremely proud of him.

I would like to make it clear while I'm on the topic of faith that I am not one of those Christians who checked her brain at the door. It is very important to learn that if any faith group tries to get you to believe through manipulation or coercion that you run like heck out of there.

Jesus never manipulates anyone. You always have the choice to say no. There is no force or obligation involved. There is an invitation…because God loves each of us. My forever prayer is that my children and grandchildren will choose to seek our Lord and their lives will be strengthened and blessed because of that choice.

I also vowed never to practice what some folks call "concussion theology" (that's where you beat someone over the head with the Bible). I prefer that my shared life experiences will be enough evidence to show that God is indeed alive and well today. St. Francis said, "Preach the Gospel at all times, if necessary…use words." I believe our world would be a better place today if we each put that bit of wisdom into practice.

The weeks faded into months after my father ended our relationship. The phone rang and I knew there was someone on the other end of the line, although no one spoke any words. I had a sense it was my father calling to hear my voice just to connect in whatever way he felt he could. Sometimes, I waited on the phone in silence. Other times, I told whoever was on the line that I understood. There were also times I got angry and told the caller to grow a spine and have some courage to talk to me. Finally, the calls were less frequent because after a while, I simply hung up.

My support groups for survivors of sexual abuse and codependency were avenues of healing. I felt oddly more real when I heard other people share their stories of healing and hope on their journey. I knew I was not alone. When someone in a meeting talked about physical abuse, I thought to myself, *At least I didn't have any of that kind of thing going on.* As soon as I would say those words, the denial would lift and memories of physical abuse would rise to the surface. I always wondered why I was able to pick up hot pans or keep my hands in hot water without much notice. Then I remembered my birth mother holding my hands over the stove burners to punish me when I did something wrong. As difficult as that was to remember, it explained my high tolerance for physical pain. Another puzzle piece fell into place.

There were other memories that surfaced over the years, most of them painful. Much like a splinter rising to the surface of the skin, a memory was exposed and healed. After I recalled the memory and grieved the pain, the less hold it had on me emotionally. As I said before, anyone who tried to negate my memories cannot explain how I was healing from something they claim I must have imagined. I was in fact healing from wounds that were emotional, physical, sexual, and spiritual. God took my shattered soul and spirit and put me back together again.

It isn't necessary to share all the details of my abuse. That is not the purpose for this book. God turned to good what others meant for evil those many years ago. There is a saying that goes something like this, "If it doesn't kill you, it will make you stronger." Faith is made stronger through trials. Little did I realize how strong God was growing my faith.

19

Earthquake

I did my best to move on and live life without any contact with my father, and then the Northridge earthquake hit Southern California on January 17, 1994. Although I had not communicated with my father, I still cared about him. I knew the earthquake most likely had an impact because his home was located close to the epicenter. I also knew it was quite possible Madge still had control over my father and would not let him speak to me directly, so I contacted my half-brother to check on my father's welfare.

Joe was surprised to hear from me but reassured me that my father was safe because he and Madge had moved to Colorado to be closer to the family. Since I had not communicated with them, I had no idea my father was now living in Colorado. Over the next couple of years, I stayed in touch with Joe. He informed me in early 1996 that my father was quite ill with Alzheimer's disease and was living in a nursing home.

It took every ounce of courage to contact Madge and tell her I wanted to see my father. I assured her that I was not coming to Colorado to cause any problems, but I had a right to see him. I was firm in my plans, and she must have been convinced that I meant no harm. After all, I had done as she wanted and that was to disappear and leave them alone. She agreed to my visit, but felt the need to tell me my father was so far into his Alzheimer's disease that he did not even remember who Joe was. She added, "He certainly won't remember who you are." For whatever reason, she had a passive aggressive way of making sure I understood I was still persona non grata.

Dennis stayed with the kids who were now twelve and fourteen years old, while I traveled alone to Colorado. I prayed and asked for God's mercy, safety, and wisdom for the journey. In one of my prayer times, God said, "You will be reconciled to your father." I held on to that promise as I traveled to see my father, possibly for the last time.

The final flight of my journey was a bit frightening because the airplane was a small puddle jumper. I nearly swallowed my tongue when the co-pilot asked me to move my feet because he wanted to close the door! Only a thin curtain hung between the passenger cabin and the cockpit, and when it opened, I could see through the cockpit window. When I got on the plane, I looked to my right and sitting directly across from me was a pastor wearing his collar. I took that as a sign that the tiny propeller plane would take off and land safely.

My half-brother's small town was at least an hour from the airport. This trip was not starting out the way I hoped because my luggage didn't arrive with me. I rented a car and drove to my brother's small town at the base of a mountain.

Joe was very sympathetic and helpful in delivering my lost luggage. He gently warned me that our father was not in very good shape and most likely would not recognize me. Janice, one of his sisters, worked as a server at a restaurant near the motel. She invited me to come early to the restaurant to talk. We talked at length about how I found my father. She was intrigued and asked many questions. As an adopted person herself, she wanted to know every detail of how I found him. Madge's fear of one of her girls locating a birth parent seemed on the edge of coming true. Janice shared stories with me of how Madge punished her when she was a child by making her get down on her hands and knees and eat out of the dog bowl when she accidentally spilled her dinner on the floor. I immediately felt a sense of comradery with her and what we both endured at the hands of mothers who were wounded themselves. Her faith was another common bond, and she said she would be praying for me while I visited our father.

The next day was a mixture of miracle, grace, and grief. Joe and Jen gave me a ride to the nursing home. Madge was already there with Joe's little boy who was no more than two years old. He was playing with his grandma's watch and had dropped it in the rocky flowerbed. They were both searching for it when we arrived.

That morning I asked God to help Madge see that I was not her enemy. I wanted to heal our relationship. As we waited to go into the nursing home, my eye caught a sparkle in the flowerbed. I reached down and picked up her watch, placed it carefully in her hand, and didn't say a word. Maybe she had prayed for healing, too, because in that moment, she seemed to soften toward me just a bit.

My father was in a wheelchair in the front room as we entered. Madge and Joe knew it was important for me to have time alone with him, so they continued down the hall. Dad was worn and fragile and bent over. He was dozing and barely aware of his surroundings. I knelt down and took his shaky hand in mine. I put my other hand under his chin and leaned close to him as I gently lifted his head to help him look into my eyes. "Dad, it's me…Cindy…your daughter. I want you to know that I love you."

A light came to his eyes and he lifted my hand to his lips and softly kissed it and said, "Oh yes!"

God whispered, "You have been reconciled to your father."

"He didn't know who you were, did he," Madge snapped. Her words were not a question but rather a statement of fact.

"I believe he did." She knew something happened. I was tearful but smiling and very much at peace. My father was more at peace, too. She was obviously upset with this reunion and needed to reclaim her power by barking orders at the nurses.

Joe was quiet as we got in the car. He glanced at me in the rearview mirror. He could tell it was an emotional visit and assumed our father did not recognize me. I didn't tell him what actually happened. I felt like a big sister who needed to protect the tender heart of her little brother. I knew I had said good-bye to my father for the last time. I turned away from his view and let my tears fall. Two months later, my father passed away.

20

The Funeral

The funeral was on March 12. Joe said he knew it might be difficult for me to make it to Colorado on such short notice but wanted me to know the time and place of the service.

Our God is always taking care of us and knows our needs even before we express them. My relationship with my Lord had grown so intimate by this time, the first thing I did in my deep grief and financial lack was to get on my knees and pray. I told God if there was any possibility for me to go to the funeral, I knew He would make a way.

I had not been on my knees praying for very long before the phone rang. The call was from my school district office. They sent me a check the previous month that was much larger than I expected. I had not cashed it because I was certain they made an error in their calculations. The woman on the phone said, "I am returning your call and wanted to let you know we underpaid you on a previous check. The extra amount you received on your recent check is accurate." God's grace overwhelmed me when the check equaled exactly what I needed for my plane ticket to Colorado! God provides and is gracious and full of mercy.

I didn't know how my father's family would receive me. It was the second time I saw Janice and the first time I met Joe's sister Laura, who still lived in California. I felt comfortable with Joe and Janice. Laura was a different story. She was not at all welcoming toward me. Looking back on it, I could see she was envious. I know from experience how difficult it is to be an adopted child and not know one's history or genetic connection in this world. Then to have someone suddenly show up, related by blood to the only father she ever knew, must have been even more difficult. She made it clear, much like her mother had, that I was not part of the family. I hoped and prayed there would be no drama at my father's funeral.

I stayed with Janice and her husband in their beautiful spacious home and was grateful to have their guest room for the time I was in Colorado. While I was there, I found myself letting go in many ways. I knew I needed to let go of my frustration with Madge. She was grieving the loss of her husband and the father of her children.

I was the long-lost daughter who at one point was the baby in the family. Now I was my father's eldest child. I was nervous on the way to the memorial service. As I walked in the door, there was an audible gasp and whispers from the people who were already seated. They were staring at me as they clearly saw a resemblance to my father. The same wide-set eyes, the same shape in our faces. I was without a doubt, my father's daughter. The family sat in the front of the little chapel as I took a seat in the row behind them.

Joe was gentle and kind and so much like our father. He knelt down, leaned close to me, and asked if I wanted to sit with the family in the front row. I told him I was fine, but I was very grateful for his invitation. His caring efforts to include me meant so much in that time of grief.

I don't remember much of the service. I was doing everything I could to hold back the pain and loss…and the anger. I was angry with Madge for causing my father to disappear from my life. My father and I reunited after thirty years, and I blamed her when he cut off our relationship. The reality was, I grieved a lifetime of losses that day.

As the service ended, people quietly left the chapel and I walked slowly up to my father's casket. I wanted to be near him one last time. I couldn't hold myself together any longer and broke down in sobs. An arm wrapped around my shoulders. It was Laura. She apologized to me and admitted she was jealous. She confessed she had hated me with a passion but was sorry for that now. She could see that I truly was his daughter. I hugged her for a long time, thanked her for her apology, and told her I understood and held no hard feelings toward her.

We drove to the cemetery and laid my father to rest under a majestic tree. This time I sat in the front row with the rest of the family. The cold Colorado wind cut through me like a knife as Laura sat next to me and cried. I felt a strength that was not mine and put my arm around her. In spite of my grief, I felt stronger and more real than I had ever felt in my entire life. The branches of the trees swayed in the icy wind as the military gun salute echoed through the cemetery. I believe my father knew I had come home to him. I also knew he had come home to God and was finally at peace. I think Madge felt God's peace, too. Both the obituary and the memorial program included Gayle and me as his daughters. It took a great deal of humility for Madge to acknowledge that truth in such a public way.

God reconciled me to my father and enabled me to help lift the pain and anger from his family. My father's prayers were answered in that time of forgiveness and healing for all of us. This is the amazing grace of God.

The sun set behind the snowcapped mountains and the airplane cabin lights flickered on as I drifted between what felt like a gaping hole in my heart and a sense of peace at the end of a very long chapter in my life.

21

Romans 8:28

*M*any difficult memories surfaced as I continued my journey of healing after my father's death. I was a wife, mother, and a teacher and needed to focus on daily life. Some days I was curled up in a fetal position on my bedroom floor, barely able to function as I recalled the painful memories. God provided strength through His grace to help me manage my healing and recovery in spite of the expectations in my various life roles.

My healing journey affected my entire family. I'm sure there were times when I couldn't meet their needs while remembering painful childhood abuse. I was too overwhelmed to be physically or emotionally available to them, and I am deeply sorry for that. There isn't much I could have done about it. Over the years, I have learned that self-forgiveness is often more difficult than forgiving others.

God provided the right people at the right time to help me heal and process the immense amount of anger and pain I carried. My dear friend Jodi is a healer, and I called her Toto because she led the way.

One day Jodi collided with a man holding camera equipment as she rushed to catch a flight. Her briefcase fell open and scattered the contents on the floor. She had some of my drawings with her because she planned to use them at a conference where she was speaking about ritual abuse. The man she ran in to was making a documentary about a type of abuse I endured, and that is satanic ritual abuse.

I should explain that as I processed my memories, I recalled horrific abuse from age three to five. At that young age, I did not have the words I needed to express the pain and horror of my trauma, but the images were there…so I drew them. The best way to explain it is that a part of me felt very young and vulnerable and drawing the pictures felt safer.

One day I bit another child in my kindergarten class. My teacher knew I was upset and told me it was not okay to bite, but I could draw about why I was upset. That was another saving grace because I didn't think I was breaking any cult rules as I drew my feelings. I found a loophole in the cult's "don't talk" rule. The cult told me not to talk about what they did to me, but they never said I couldn't draw.

It just so happened the man with the camera equipment worked for Word Inc., a Christian publishing company on the East Coast. They were making a documentary about satanic ritual abuse. He saw my drawings as he was helping Jodi put her briefcase back together and asked about them. They were on the same flight, and as they traveled, they discussed both his documentary project and her healing conference. She gave him my contact information, and he asked me to be a part of the documentary series called *American Exposé: Rituals of Rebellion*.[6] That exposé helped many doctors, nurses, and counselors understand more about cults and ritual abuse. Many professionals watched the documentary and were educated in how to help people ritually abused as children. God was, in fact, turning the stuff of my childhood into fertilizer. That is just one of many examples of coincidences (God instances really) that happened in my life. God was working all things for the good.

22

Flying Monkeys
and Scary Castles

*M*y healing progressed far enough that I was able to share my journey with other survivors of abuse. God equipped me to provide healing tips and guidance for counselors and therapists. I also educated helping professionals who were directly assisting abuse survivors, especially survivors of satanic ritual abuse. In addition, I helped survivors online through a Christian website. By now the internet, email, and websites were becoming the norm for information sharing. The number of people who reached out to me because of a poem I shared at a Survivorship conference in the early 1990s, or a comment made on a webpage for survivors of abuse was amazing. What was even more amazing is the "God instances" continued.

In addition to the documentary, I participated in a local television news story and shared my experiences and some of my drawings. The news team agreed to hide my face to protect me. The phone lines in the newsroom immediately lit up with calls from other survivors thanking the news team for running the story. As controversial as it was to run a story about satanic ritual abuse, the number of people who called the station and confirmed the reality of that type of abuse was overwhelming.

Many callers shared similar experiences of cult abuse.

There were other opportunities for me to help abuse survivors. I shared part of my story in the book *Breaking the Circle of Satanic Ritual Abuse: Recognizing and Discovering Hidden Trauma* by Daniel Ryder C.C.D.C., L.S.W.[7] That chapter was on the topic of cult harassment and the backlash of exposing the cult and their practice of ritual abuse. Truth telling was not what members of the satanic cult wanted, but my truth telling helped more people become free from the pain and control the cult used to keep their victims bound in fear for most of their lives.

Yet another God instance occurred. I checked my email messages one day and came across an email with a subject line that read, "Decision Today." I assumed it was a sales pitch for me to make a decision to buy a product they were selling, so I pressed delete. I was absolutely certain I deleted the message, but oddly the email was still in my in-box. I opened the email mostly out of curiosity. It was an invitation from the Rev. Billy Graham ministry *Decision Today* radio show. They wanted to interview me about my Christian website for abuse survivors. I never sought this attention nor expected the website to draw much notice. I did the interview and a few other interviews, which helped several more people on their healing journey.

Another lesson from scripture became real for me during this time. It is from 2 Corinthians 1:3–4 and speaks clearly about what I was experiencing: "Praise be to the God and Father of our Lord Jesus Christ, the Father of compassion and the God of all comfort, who comforts us in all our troubles, so that we can comfort those in any trouble with the comfort we ourselves receive from God."

I know God helped others through my transformed suffering. I cannot explain my healing journey more clearly than this. There were many "God instances" that happened along the path of my healing journey, and I know without a doubt that God walked with me every step of the way.

I never thought the help I provided would bring about such a violent reaction from the cult. Suddenly I started being harassed for exposing their methods of mind control and programming. I did not realize the cult was as active as it was when I was a child, perhaps even more so.

The cult did not like me talking. They also didn't like how I was able to break free from their programming. I figured out the programming based on memories, as well as God-given dreams that revealed the secrets of the enemy satan. (I don't ever capitalize satan's name because he does not deserve it.) Scripture is clear about the difference between God's agenda and satan's agenda in John 10:10: "The thief comes only to steal and kill and destroy; I have come that they may have life, and have it to the full."

The apostle Paul teaches us how to protect ourselves ourselves from the enemy's agenda in Ephesians 6:11–13:

Put on the full armor of God, so that you can take your stand against the devil's schemes. For our struggle is not against flesh and blood, but against the rulers, against the authorities, against the powers of this dark world and against the spiritual forces of evil in the heavenly realms. Therefore put on the full armor of God, so that when the day of evil comes, you may be able to stand your ground, and after you have done everything, to stand.

Shortly after the articles and news stories aired, local cult members aggressively harassed me. I was exposing their dark secrets to the light of day, and they wanted to teach me a lesson. They also used me as an example as to what would happen to any survivor who breaks the "don't talk" rule.

Cult members followed me to church and sat near me in order to threaten or re-program me. One of the more insidious cult programs (when I was a young child) was to tell me "Nobody would hurt me." The cult actually programmed me to believe that a person named "Nobody" was the person hurting me. That way, if I broke free of the cult and someone tried to reassure me by saying, "Nobody will hurt you," the helper unknowingly triggered the threat that a "bad guy" named, "Nobody" would hurt me if I sought help or exposed the cult. As scary as that was, it was a breakthrough for me because that program was directly connected to suicidal programming, which, simply put, if I started to remember or reveal the cult's secrets, I would automatically try to kill myself.

The more I talked, the more the harassment increased. I was leaving my dentist's office a few days after I spoke to school counselors about how to recognize cult abuse. A woman was sitting in the middle of the stairway reading a Bible. It was obvious she would have to move out of the way for anyone who wanted to get to the parking lot. As soon as I stepped past the woman on the stairwell, she left and got into her car. I made note of the make of her car and license plate number.

My head throbbed and I felt sick and dizzy by the time I reached the parking lot. My dental appointment was a simple cleaning and nothing the dental hygienist did would cause such a bad headache. Fortunately, my house was only a short distance from the dentist's office. I was so dizzy I lay down on my bed waiting for the dizziness to pass, but I fell asleep. No one else was home at the time. There was an odd bruise on my arm when I woke up, and I couldn't remember hitting my arm on anything. It felt like I'd been given a shot of some kind.

You may be thinking at this point, "Yeah, right, I think you are just making this up." I guarantee you I am not. Daniel Ryder's research and interviews of other survivors is eerily similar to mine. I shared these experiences with Dennis, and he was skeptical of the harassment I was describing. He thought

I was paranoid or had an over active imagination. In spite of his doubt, I became more vigilant after that experience and paid closer attention to people around me. I also tried not to attend church alone. If they followed me to one church, I went to a different church the next Sunday. I was not about to let the cult intimidate me into silence. God made me stubborn for a reason. Ezekiel 3:9 says, "I will make your forehead like the hardest stone, harder than flint. Do not be afraid of them or terrified by them, though they are a rebellious people."

The challenge of overcoming cult abuse is reversing the programming deeply imbedded in the victim. The cult twisted everything. What's up is down, what's right is wrong, what's good is evil. I had to unlearn the teaching the cult indoctrinated me with at such a young, impressionable age. I am a survivor. More than that, I am a thriver, and God used everything I endured to strengthen my faith and courage.

One afternoon, the woman from the dental office parked her car in front of our house. I warned both kids that if they ever saw that car near our house, they should stay away. They were playing at their friend's house down the street. Back then, we didn't have cell phones. William saw the car parked in front of our house and ran inside the neighbor's house to call and warn me not to open the door. Unfortunately, I was already opening the door while the phone rang. The next thing I knew, I felt sick and dizzy and the woman was driving away.

The harassment occurred several times and in various places. That is, until the day they came to the door again around noon when I was home alone. This time it was two different women claiming to be members of a religious organization. They said they wanted to give me a magazine. I carefully opened the door, and suddenly I was sliding down the wall to the floor. Dennis occasionally came home from work for lunch. That day he happened to walk in the back door as I was sliding down the wall. He could no longer deny the assaults or excuse it as my imagination. I showed him a very distinct puncture wound in my arm. Being the scientist that he is he took a video of the wound as evidence. Dennis finally believed me. I learned later from a cult expert, that cult members injected survivors with trace amounts of poison to scare the survivor into silence. They also used these assaults to scare other cult survivors.

One survivor I knew was more public about her abuse, and the cult had information about her personal life and family. She was going to speak at an abuse survivor's conference on the steps of the state capitol. Cult members threatened her and said her children would be hurt if she gave her presentation.

In the meantime, I made notes and documented license plate numbers and kept specific details on cult members who threatened me. The last thing a cult member wants is to have their identity revealed. The word "occult" means "secret." I told my friend if she didn't want to speak at the conference, I would speak for her. After I read her poems on the steps of the capitol, I told the crowd, "To anyone who may be associated with the cult, we will not be silenced! I'm reading this poem for a friend who was threatened. You need to know that I have information about you, and my attorney has a copy of that information. If I go down…YOU go down!"

I didn't care what happened to me. In hindsight, I recognize I had an edge of bravado. I was tired of the harassment and decided I'd had enough. My threat to the cult members in the crowd at the capitol that day was definitely a risk, but the cult harassment decreased after that.

Psalm 54:4 summarizes how I survived and have lived to tell my story. The Word of God is living, not just in the past, but also for today. One of my favorite lines from this psalm is "Surely God is my help; the Lord is the one who sustains me."

23

On my Own with God

The entire ordeal over several months, in addition to my healing which was now into years, took a toll on my marriage. Dennis had no idea how to cope with my childhood abuse as it oozed to the surface. I'm sure there were many times he felt abandoned in our marriage because I was either doing a television interview or helping a survivor online or dealing with post-traumatic stress myself. This is not what he signed up for when he married me. Of course, the more challenging life became, the more I prayed and sought God. God was my sanctuary from the horrendous memories and the cult harassment.

Ultimately, my relationship with God was the biggest dividing factor in our marriage. Dennis did not share the same beliefs, and unfortunately, that was the final nail in the coffin of our relationship. I believe we would have made it through those challenging times if we had a shared faith and been able to pray and ask God for help together. A shared faith is often the glue that will hold a marriage together when life gets tough.

The divorce was certainly difficult. I did not want to hurt Dennis or my children, but we were fighting all the time. My therapy, the harassment, and the time I spent helping other survivors was a drain on both of us, and we weren't able to let go of the pain we experienced over that time. The tension became so thick I felt increasingly hopeless and sometimes suicidal. As a Christian, I did not believe in divorce. I thought I was supposed to stay with him forever, but that is not what happened. He told me I was not the person he married and that was true. I was stronger because of what I endured, and I was no longer afraid of conflict. The person I was when I married Dennis was not the person I had become over my healing years. I was no longer placating or codependent in our relationship. I finally found my courage and my voice.

The first few years after our divorce were difficult to say the least. I was a single woman with very little income. My kids were still in junior high school, and I ended my teaching job just prior to our divorce because I felt a call to train in the art of Spiritual Direction. The best definition I have ever heard of a Spiritual Director or Spiritual Companion, as I prefer to say, is from the book *Companions in Christ* by Marjorie Thompson et.al. Thompson says, "A Spiritual Companion can 'listen us' into clarity."[8]

After my work in ministering to survivors of abuse, as well as the numerous support groups I attended throughout my healing, I developed (or honed rather) an ability to listen deeply to another person. A spiritual companion doesn't just listen to the person, s/he also listens to the Divine, Holy Spirit, God (or whatever name for God you use) while being present to the directee. Unlike counseling, which is a one-to-one relationship, spiritual direction includes God.

I held several different jobs in the years after my divorce. Amazingly, God was weaving them together into a beautiful fabric to prepare me for a greater work that was to come. I worked as a church office administrator and later as an administrative assistant at a spiritual formation center. I completed my training in the art of spiritual direction and became a part-time spiritual director. It was during this time that I felt the greatest financial challenge because I purchased a car and no longer had a full-time income.

Again, after prayer for direction and discernment, God spoke to me in a dream and provided for me in astounding ways. God never abandoned me and He wasn't about to abandon me now. This was my dream:

I am driving my car and it begins to stall. Before it stalls completely, I pull over into a temporary parking spot and a security guard tells me I cannot park there because it is not for permanent parking. I ask him, "May I just park here temporarily since my car has broken down?" Just then, I see a man from my church in my rearview mirror. As he gets closer to my car, my car starts again.

God still works miracles today. The man in my dream called me the next week. His wife had passed away after a long illness. He had a sixth-grade daughter and another daughter in junior high school. He told me he needed a nanny for his youngest daughter and heard from someone at church that I was looking for a job. His very words were, "It is only temporary, but I was wondering if you would be interested in working as my nanny." God worked through His people to provide for my needs. The miracle didn't end there. The man told me he would have to write my first check in advance because he needed to use his wife's social security money immediately or he would lose it.

God was incredibly gracious during the lean months. A couple that I knew from my teaching job came to my office one afternoon. They said they were praying about it and offered to let me live in their extra bedroom...rent-free! I lived with them for six months and then I was able to afford my own apartment. By then, I was working three part-time jobs as an administrative assistant, spiritual director, and nanny. Holding down three jobs was a bit frenetic, but God worked it all for the good and continued to provide a light to my path.

It was no accident when I discovered I had a "call within a call." Each time I went to my office at the spiritual formation center, I encountered a homeless person sleeping on the steps of the church. Frequently, I sat with them and listened to their stories of homelessness and their heart's desire. There was a remarkable amount of grace to listen to them with God's compassion as they shared their painful stories. I was, in fact, finding myself in the position of spiritual companion to homeless individuals. I continued to hold this developing position in prayer, asking God for a deeper understanding and direction for my life.

Then I had another dream. The dream was quite unusual because it was in color. I seldom dream in color so this was definitely a dream I remembered. In the dream...

a man is playing a violin on a street corner near a café. He is wearing a court jester's suit and multicolored hat with a bell on top. His violin case is on the ground and he is collecting money as he plays. The message with the dream was that the man in the jester's suit was homeless, and I was not to fear him. I was to trust that he would bless me.

The following weekend I traveled to the coast with my friend Jennifer. She and I were meeting her father for lunch at a restaurant near his home. As we waited for him on the café patio, I talked with Jennifer about some possible job changes and told her I was growing weary of juggling my various part-time jobs. I shared what was on my heart, including my dream. All of a sudden, we heard a violin playing. I turned around and there on the street corner stood a man in a court jester's suit wearing a multicolored hat with a bell on the top! He was homeless and opened his violin case hoping for a bit of cash.

Jennifer turned to me with a big grin on her face and said, "I think you are meant to do something with the homeless!"

After I returned from our trip, I looked in the newspaper for jobs and found one listed for a resource staff member at a homeless shelter. I applied and got the job. That was the beginning of a multitude of blessings.

24

A Stand for Justice

*M*y work at the homeless shelter was both challenging and enlightening. My interactions with the majority of homeless individuals was easy and comfortable. That was in itself, surprising. I didn't have any fear of the folks who accessed the shelter. However, the director ran the shelter with an iron hand and was, in my opinion, extremely rude to the homeless people who frequented there. She was miserly in handing out needed donations, laundry soap, and general supplies. Initially I assumed she didn't have enough donations from the community and she needed to be careful with her distribution. Then I began to see something else.

She was giving me a tour of the facility during my training and as she walked through the long-term shelter where the more permanent residents stayed, she took a loaf of bread and some raisins off a resident's food shelf and proudly announced that she was going to make her husband some bread pudding. Stealing food from homeless individuals was not okay with me.

I wasn't at my job very long before I saw more of that sort of behavior from the director. As a Christian, I could not condone her stealing and throwing people out of the shelter if they complained about the way they were treated. I also noticed holiday donations distributed to people who were not homeless.

Many people came to the shelter during the holidays. When I asked them how I could assist them, they said they were there to see the director. There was a frequent number of visitors going to the director's office and then leaving the shelter with holiday donations. Her friends and family and perhaps even her neighbors were receiving the donations meant for homeless individuals. In the meantime, homeless guests were freezing and were begging me for warm clothes and blankets.

I tried to stay focused on my job and follow her directions. She spent hours locked in her office talking with someone on the phone or chatting with friends who would drop in. They visited for a while and then left with new coats or hand-made scarves and even portable televisions. Her office door remained closed when they were visiting. That is when I decided to take a stand for justice. I handed out socks and blankets without waiting for her approval. If I waited for her to do her job, the homeless guests would have frozen to death.

During this time, I often heard a song in my mind as a homeless individual approached my office for supplies. The song was "Sing Alleluia to the Lord." I didn't hear the song with every homeless guest, just some of them. It was as if God was tapping me on the shoulder and reminding me to "pray for this one." Another guest came to my door and I wouldn't hear anything. Then the next person stepped up to the door and I once again heard God say, "This one…pray for this one." and the song would float through my mind, "Sing Alleluia to the Lord."

The pattern continued for a few weeks, until the day I heard the song again. It was louder this time. I looked up into the battered face of a homeless man who had been assaulted with a bat as he slept outside. His eyes were black and blue. His nose, jaw, and several teeth broken. He had his jaw wired shut to keep his jawbone and remaining teeth in place. I stifled a gasp but couldn't hold back the tears or ignore the lump in my throat. My heart ached for this man. I gave him what he needed and touched his hand. He nodded his head in thanks… and in that very moment, his face transformed into the face of Jesus. I caught my breath as he walked away and I stood there in holy awe. God was here among the least of these. The words from Matthew 25:40 came to me then. "The King will reply, 'Truly I tell you, whatever you did for one of the least of these brothers and sisters of mine, you did for me.'"

As the weeks passed, I grew more and more frustrated with the director and the blatant theft and abuse I witnessed. The final straw of the job was when a homeless man with a spirit as gentle as a dove arrived a couple minutes late to the shelter. There are rules about what time he should have arrived in order to keep his reserved bed. He told me that it was the anniversary of his mother's death, and he took the bus to the next city to meet his brother who was having a very difficult time on the first anniversary of her passing. The bus was late when he returned and he did not make it back to the shelter in time. He was five minutes late.

The next morning the director stormed out of her office, threw a green garbage bag in my face and growled, "Throw him out of here and make sure he doesn't come back." I escorted this gentle soul of a man to his room, and he quietly put his meager belongings into the green garbage bag I held.

"They don't know how to take you in here, but they sure know how to throw you out," he said softly. He knew I was upset. "Don't worry, Cindy, God will find a way for me."

I knew I could not keep working at the shelter after that, and I prayed for God to show me what I was supposed to do.

I was scared, yet knew I could not tolerate the mistreatment of these poor homeless people. I also knew if I gave up the job, I could become homeless myself. The next day I began to keep written documentation of what the director was doing, including asking me to falsify data on the computer. I turned my documentation over to her boss and the board of directors and prayed God show me my next step.

25

Saul's Dream

I have learned to trust God by faith on my life journey. I knew if I asked for God's help, I would receive it. Although, often times God's answers came in ways I never expected.

It was December, and more homeless people were coming to the shelter to escape the cold and receive donations. Donations came in the door from local churches and other compassionate individuals, so the door to the shelter was frequently open.

One morning a couple of weeks before Christmas, a short Hispanic man walked in the door. He didn't say much but cocked his head from side to side, blinking his eyes as if to clear his vision. I thought that perhaps he didn't speak English, so I said, "*Hola ¿Como esta?*"

His boots scraped the floor as he moved closer to my office doorway. He pointed at me and asked, "You speak Spanish?"

"*Muy poco.*"

He glanced down the hallway and noticed the director's closed door and waved for me to follow him out to the porch. A volunteer took over the distribution of donations, and I followed the man outside.

He started speaking excitedly in broken English. "My name is Saul. I had a dream about you, you were in my dream." He repeated, "I don't know you…you were in my dream!" He glanced around to make sure others were not listening and continued. "We were driving in a Blazer on the freeway. We were going up to Oregon and it was so beautiful! We were flying over the freeway." He stepped closer and with tears in his eyes said, "I woke up from the dream and thought of my dead wife, made the sign of the cross and asked God, 'Why would you give me this beautiful dream God, I am just a homeless man?'"

I stood on holy ground in those few moments. This man had a faith and relationship with God that was tangible. He asked me again, "Tell me why God would give me such a dream."

"I think, Saul, that God gave you that dream for me. God has just answered my prayer for direction!"

His eyebrows raised suddenly as he discreetly nodded his head toward the shelter. The door was open and he saw the director coming down the hallway. "You better go do your job."

I turned around to thank him…he had disappeared.

The dream Saul shared with me was still on my mind when I went home that night. I prayed about it and asked God what the dream meant. Without hesitation, I received the answer in my spirit. "Blaze (riding in a Blazer) a new trail (the Oregon Trail) the Free Way. (The truth shall set you free.)" God was calling me to minister to homeless guests in the community with the freedom of Christ. I was to pray with them, hold them in God's compassionate heart, and stir up the churches to "do" as Matthew 25 so clearly states. I didn't know it until much later, but the name Saul is a Hebrew baby name meaning, "Asked for or inquired of God."

26

Grace in Action

I quit my job at the shelter just before Christmas that year. I had no income or health insurance. During this time, a local church heard several complaints from homeless people and others who were concerned about the treatment they received from the shelter director. The church decided to hold a meeting to address those concerns. Two of the homeless guests asked me to attend that meeting to support them as they shared what they knew about the director. The homeless guests wanted the church leadership to do something about the injustice. The church held several meetings to learn details so they would know how to respond to the concerns of homeless people. I collected sleeping bags, tarps, and blankets and stored them in the trunk of my car.

This ad hoc church group held several more meetings, and I attended as many as I could. Yet I was exasperated with all the talk and no action. I probably insulted some people at a meeting one rainy night. I shared what I knew about the local shelter and the director. Then I told them I could no longer just *talk* about doing something. I wanted to take action! I had tarps and new sleeping bags in my car that I needed to deliver to people who were trying to sleep out in the rain.

I knew I could not wait for that church or any church to

hold meeting after meeting to decide how to help those who were less fortunate. I realize there is a reason to be clear about needed details, but sometimes holding numerous meetings is simply a convenient way to procrastinate in order to avoid actually doing what may be quite challenging or controversial. My heart ached for the people who struggled out on the street. Many of them slept in the park directly across from that church. I knew that holding more meetings wasn't helping them at all. I was done with the lack of action. I walked out of the meeting and didn't look back.

There was another homeless man outside the church pacing back and forth in the rain, anxiously smoking a cigarette. He was waiting to talk to his homeless friends who were still at the meeting. I was a little wary because he seemed to have some mental health issues so I headed to my car with the intention of delivering some of the supplies I had in my trunk. Suddenly, he stepped in front of me. He got up in my face and matter-of-factly said, "You are a truth teller!" I had never met this homeless man and his revelation unnerved me. He thanked me for going to the meeting and then continued with wide eyes and his bony finger sharply poking my shoulder. "Do you know what they do to truth tellers? They crucify them. This church will crucify you!"

Little did I know the man I thought might be mentally ill, was also a truth teller and likely prophetic. Thirteen years later the very words this man spoke to me that cold rainy night came true.

27

Grace House

Several churches in town had homeless people sleeping on their porches. Church leadership wanted to help, but they were not convinced that giving the homeless person money was actually helping. One day I walked into a local church and introduced myself to the administrative assistant. I told her I wanted to help the people who were sleeping at their church. "If there is anything I can do for you, I am a liaison between homeless people and the churches, so please don't hesitate to call me." I think my statement surprised both of us because it was the first time I had ever said it. God was making it clear out of my own mouth, exactly what I was supposed to be doing! The administrative assistant seemed just as surprised by my introduction because she jumped up from behind her desk and squealed with joy. "This is exactly what we have been praying for!" She introduced me to one of the pastors, who immediately wrote me a check so I could buy a pager, and that was the beginning of a local Christian ministry to homeless individuals.

With a handful of volunteers, we managed to feed, minister to, and provide donations to homeless individuals while preventing other homeless folks from receiving funds to purchase alcohol or drugs. Over time, the ministry became a liaison between churches and homeless individuals who genuinely needed a hand up rather than just a hand out. God was indeed leading the way.

The ministry grew and changed over the years. God's presence was evident in so many ways. Homeless individuals received warm clothes and much needed supplies donated by various church congregations. The churches supported our nonprofit ministry, which grew from handing out lunches and donations from the trunk of my car, to offering a rest and respite in the parking lot of one church, in the fellowship room of another, and a Bible study at yet another church. It was incredible to see God go before us and offer opportunities for congregation members to learn how to minister and serve as agents of God's grace to those most in need.

It didn't take long for the ministry to outgrow the trunk of my car. We purchased a van from one of our church partners and used it to carry the many donations from church to church. We informed our homeless guests of the schedule when we would hand out donations.

As the ministry grew, so did my weariness. I continued to work part-time as a nanny and minister to homeless individuals. I also served as the administrator of the ministry. The paperwork and documentation to secure our non-profit status still needed to be completed. Most of the administrative work happened once I got home at the end of the day. The ministry also included late night visits to emergency rooms and frequent calls from pastors who needed our assistance. I was growing weary of the roving nature of the ministry. In addition, gas prices to fill the tank of our large van were increasing. The fact is we quickly outgrew the model we were using. I was financially struggling too. Some weeks I lived on bags of potatoes for food because funds were short. Yet God provided for our homeless guests and me in miraculous ways.

Not surprisingly, I enjoyed my potato meals!

It took some time to build up the nonprofit to a point where it could sustain the ministry to our homeless guests. By the way, we called them "guests" because that is what they were. I refused to allow our volunteers to refer to them as "the homeless" because that dehumanizes them in many respects. I was determined to include them in whatever way we could, to have no separation between volunteers and homeless guests.

As I said, I was struggling financially as a single woman. The board of directors and I prayed for discernment of God's next step for the ministry. Shortly after we prayed, our volunteer administrator received a call from a member of his church. She asked him how much rent we paid for our office. He chuckled when he told her we were much too small and too new to have an office. He told her I did my work out of my apartment and my car. The woman explained that she had received an inheritance from a family member. When she was praying about what to do with the money, the word "rent" came to mind, and she thought of our ministry. When he told her that we did not rent an office, she asked, "What does her apartment rent cost?" He didn't know so he guessed at a sum and she wrote a check for ten thousand dollars! That amount carried me through the next year until our nonprofit status was official, and I could devote all of my time and energy to the ministry. I still had no health insurance, but I was not sick at all that entire year…not even with the slightest cold. Our God is faithful!

The ministry outgrew our van and my small apartment. One afternoon I drove down the road and passed a small house on the property of one of the churches. I frequently traveled this route as I drove around ministering to our homeless guests. Over a period of about two weeks, each time I passed this house I heard the words "Write a proposal." I don't know if you have ever heard this phrase before, but I refer to these repeated words as "prayer gnats" because I often try to swat them away like a gnat in my ear or I ignore them (singing la, la, la, la) to avoid actually doing what God wants me to do. God can be very persistent because of His love for each of us, especially when it comes to grace, mercy, and provision.

Finally, this instruction became so loud whenever I drove past the little house, I could no longer ignore it. I sat down one morning and wrote a proposal to the church asking to use the small house for the ministry. The church leadership unanimously approved our proposal to use the house with no rental fee. We finally had a home (sort of) for our homeless guests. We affectionately named it Grace House. We no longer traveled from church to church or carted supplies in and out of the van. We now had a permanent location where our guests could rest during the day and receive God's love and provision. The ministry was at Grace House for almost five years. We provided Christmas meals, donated gifts, and met ongoing needs of our homeless guests. Many homeless guests and volunteers experienced God on a daily basis.

We were quietly going about the work of serving our homeless guests with little attention on us, until someone suggested we advertise our ministry. That was the beginning of the end.

I believe it is never wise to desire attention if one is serving quietly. I was satisfied knowing that our homeless guests knew where to find us, but some board members did not agree. The nonprofit nature of the ministry required fundraisers and public attention. To this day, I seriously doubt the neighbors knew we were there until they read an article about the ministry in the local newspaper. Shortly after the article was printed, neighbors who were of the NIMBY (Not in My Back Yard) crowd, protested loudly to the city and church. They filed complaints about the number of homeless people the church was serving lunches to and that we were ministering to on the church property.

That church held a special city use permit because it was the first established church in the city. Ultimately, in order to keep their special permit, the church leaders signed a Memorandum of Understanding with the city to limit the number of lunches they would hand out to homeless individuals. Our board of directors and I believed we were to serve as many homeless people as God wanted to serve, even if we exceeded the arbitrary city limit.

The ministry was a separate nonprofit and collaborated with several Christian churches, not just that one. We said the church could throw us out of the house rather than turn away someone God wanted us to minister to or feed. Taking a stand and following the gospel was a risk, but it was a risk we believed God wanted us to take. By faith, we knew we were there to serve God and our homeless guests. We were not there to appease the secular government.

Sadly, that as well as other ways we (mostly me) "called the question" of that particular church, became a thorn between us. Eventually one of the church leaders tried to end my presence at Grace House. The details of the way I was treated and the stress of the entire ordeal was painful and there is no need to revisit it here. Simply put, it was time for me to stomp the dust from my feet and move on from that city and the people and ministry I so dearly loved.

In the final months of our presence at Grace House, the ministry moved to numerous other churches who graciously and warmly welcomed us. The actions taken toward me by that church pastor were in my opinion, both illegal and immoral. An attorney advised me that I had an open and shut case of both slander and libel and that I should sue the church. Some of my responses during this time were definitely not positive. However, I was not interested in pursuing litigation. Although the behavior of that pastor and other members of that church shocked me, I was too weary to invest any more of my time and energy there. Sadly, one person said, "Cindy, I was so close to going back to the church, but after seeing the way that pastor treated you, I don't think I will." That kind of statement cuts like a knife into the heart of our God.

The church, like many people, is broken and flawed. No person or group can determine the measure of God's love for you or me. Whether individual or church, we all make mistakes, and it is our Lord's forgiveness and reconciliation that will ultimately turn each of us back to grace.

I retired my service to the ministry in 2013, exactly thirteen years after the homeless man jabbed my shoulder with his bony finger and said, "This church will crucify you." In spite of all that happened and by God's strength and grace alone…I am still a truth teller.

28

Dan and New Life

I kept many journals over the years. As I read my old journals, I noticed I frequently wrote a prayer asking God for
a husband who shared my faith and would love me and not
expect me to become someone else just to satisfy his ego.

I allowed my work and daily life to get in the way of dating after my divorce from Dennis. The truth is, I was afraid
to commit to a serious relationship. I had to learn that I must
love myself before I could allow true love to grow and develop
with anyone else. God helped me learn how to love myself, to
forgive myself for the past, and to risk trusting someone again.
Trust was, and still is, a very fragile treasure in my life.

God wrote the story of how I met Dan. As an introvert,
I seldom attend events with large crowds of people unless it
relates to work. A woman from work invited me to a prayer
meeting at her church on Valentine's Day. I met Dan for the
first time at that meeting. I was not comfortable because there
were so many people in a very small space (sheer torture for
an introvert!). Apparently, I said something during the meeting that impressed Dan, and he was intrigued by my spiritual
depth (or so he says.) Then on my birthday, I attended a gathering of folks in the home of one of the church members.

On my way to the gathering, I drove on a country road

through a light rain and I recalled something my spiritual director, David Burnet, said to me. "When you align your prayers with God's will, pray with sincerity and faith and trust that God will answer your prayer...then you will see results from your prayers." That is exactly what I did. I prayed with true sincerity, "God, you are the giver of good gifts and I would like a husband for my birthday."

The home where the gathering took place was down a muddy road out in the country. It was like a barn in its layout and had a large living room where we gathered to sing and pray. There seemed to be a hundred people there, but it was probably only thirty or forty. Everyone gathered for music and a time of worship, and Dan led the whole thing. His deep love for God and his incredible ability to make God's Word come alive impressed me. It was obvious he knew God's Word, and he made it more real than I had ever experienced before. I glanced around the room and noticed that the majority of people in attendance were women, although there were also a few men. Then I heard God say, "Love, honor, and encourage this man." Dan was the only man standing near me, so I thought God wanted me to pray for him.

Now one would think I would have remembered my prayer to God with my birthday request, but I wanted to know what I was supposed to be doing for this man. I heard the words again, "Love, honor, and encourage this man." In that moment, I looked up and the window in the loft opened ever so slowly and a rainbow appeared in the sky. Everyone was in awe of the beauty of that rainbow and I immediately felt a sense of hope. It was very much what people refer to as a "God moment."

After the gathering ended, I asked Dan how I could pray for him.

"Most of my friends are praying that I get a job because I was laid off."

"Why are you looking for a job? You are doing exactly what God wants you to do right now," I said.

He was a bit startled because he was in his element during the leading of worship and teaching of God's Word. In fact, he admitted later that teaching about God was his heart's desire. I don't think there is anything that fills him with more joy than leading worship and prayer. He told me later that I saw into his soul and spirit that night. I just knew intuitively that he was doing exactly what God had called him to do in life.

God speaking direction to me, the window in the loft opening, the rainbow appearing in the sky, and my conversation with Dan, made for a very special birthday!

A couple of weeks later Dan called and asked if I would like to meet for coffee. We met and talked for two hours, but the time flew by in what seemed like only two minutes and the spark ignited. When I returned home, my friend Ann asked me where I had been. I told her that I just had coffee with my future husband. I knew God answered my heart-felt prayer.

Dan and I dated and got to know each other over the next year. He was struggling with his unemployment, and his ex-wife had lived in a separate room in their house for six years before I met him. She told him when he was laid off, that she didn't want to be married anymore and filed for divorce.

My transition away from the homeless ministry I loved was stressful and heart wrenching. God's timing of bringing Dan and I together was perfect. We leaned on God and each other through our separate trials. However, some legalistic and judgmental Christians didn't see our grace-filled relationship in the same light. The very Christians Dan led in prayer and worship ostracized both of us. The American church steeped in legalism today is one of the main reasons people avoid church all together. Sadly, many Christians miss the mark when it comes to God's grace and loving people right where they are.

Dan was different from any man I ever met. He was compassionate and caring, humble and kind. He loved God and delighted in my vocal points of view. He valued and encouraged my personal and political beliefs and did not feel threatened by my experience. He made it safe for me to be me and told me he was very happy to know the uncensored Cindy. That alone made him different from any other man I dated. I often felt I needed to curb my views with other people, not just men.

A year or more after we met, we were at the beach and Dan proposed. We both knew God brought us together, and Dan was already talking about whom to invite to our wedding before he officially asked me to marry him. God gave me the best birthday gift I could ever ask for, and I am immensely grateful to Dan for the gift of becoming his wife.

Dan had no plans and little comfort about becoming a grandpa. His son, Sean, was still in junior high school when we met. It took some adjustment after my granddaughters were born, but it didn't take long for Dan to fall in love with all four granddaughters. Today he wears his "Coolest Grandpa Ever" hat with pride and much joy.

God turned our lives around. As I look back, I remember a time when we each struggled with borderline homelessness. As I said, I lived on potatoes during the early years of the ministry so I could pay my daily expenses, and Dan borrowed money from friends to keep both Sean and him fed and housed.

Our God is a God of restoration and new life. We moved away from the city of our past, Dan became employed, and I worked at a retirement job that I absolutely loved. We combined our resources and bought a wonderful home where our granddaughters could play, splash in the wading pool, plant flowers, and celebrate Thanksgiving together. Our family has shared holidays and much laughter and love in our new home. We are truly blessed by God's grace.

29

Full Circle and
the Mysteries of God

The mother who adopted me is ninety-seven years old as I come to the end of my story. She is a strong lady and still fiercely independent in her assisted living home. The home I grew up in has long since been torn down and the canal we splashed in is buried and covered over by parking lots and large buildings. I have not driven by the old property where our house once stood. I prefer to remember it just as I described it to you.

I am still friends with a neighborhood girl almost sixty years after we first met. My friend Charlene attended my seventh birthday party shortly after my adoption. There is nothing like a life-long friendship.

Today when we meet, Charlene and I feel as though we are starting our conversation where we previously left off. Sometimes, months or even years pass before we meet again. Some friends are life-long friends. Others have moved on. Some will come back around again when you least expect them to.

I remember a little five-year-old boy in Louise's kindergarten class. Imagine my surprise when the boy's father said hello to me outside her classroom. The student who once threatened my life stood right there in front of me. I didn't know it then but several years later, he would protect me from harm. The next time I saw him I was in a park surrounded by some tough looking homeless men. I was new to my homeless work and was nervous in that setting even though another volunteer was with me. The men made some derogatory comments and were a bit menacing toward us. Very slowly, a man sitting on top of a picnic table turned around and looked at me. He lowered his sunglasses and growled at the men, "Shut up!" Then he simply said, "She's okay." More than once during the homeless ministry, this former student I taught how to read from a driver's handbook told his homeless buddies to treat me with respect.

When I left Texas, I was certain I would never return to that state. The fact is, I did return to Texas. Our small California AAUW branch decided it was time to allow men to join the organization. Much like government politics, there were splits within the national organization and some women disagreed with us. There were many organizations for men that did not allow women to participate. We believed that was discriminatory. We also believed it was hypocritical to allow only women in our organization yet complain about the same discrimination in men's organizations.

Six women from our branch created what we called "The Equity Network." This small group of women started a campaign to bring together as many states as possible to pass our anti-discrimination resolution at the national convention in Houston, Texas. Somehow, I became the spokesperson from our group. I began my presentation for the resolution in my best Texas twang, "I am honored to have been president of a new branch of AAUW when I lived in the great state of Texas." By the time we completed our networking and presented the resolution, there were yellow ribbons (the color we chose for our campaign) throughout the crowd of attendees. The resolution passed! Women can do mighty things in this world when we are determined.

I never expected part of that state to return to me. The couple who helped us adjust to Texas, moved back to California. Unfortunately, she and her husband were divorced a few years after they arrived. My friend was in her second marriage when diagnosed with early stage Parkinson's disease. Sadly, her partner did not have the courage or integrity to stick with her during those difficult first months of her diagnosis and gutlessly abandoned her.

I moved nine times in the twelve years I worked in the homeless ministry and often felt homeless myself. Through the mystery of God, my friend from Texas needed a live-in caretaker at the same time I was looking for housing again. I moved into her home and took care of her for a few years before she moved to a facility with a higher level of care. I still visit her today, and we laugh about the crazy things that happened on the various trips we took together and the delightful things our grandchildren say and do. She teaches me every day about humility and grace and is far more forgiving than I would have been. She never told her children about the emotional suffering she endured during the first few years after her divorce. She always protected her sons from her pain just to keep the peace for their sake and that of her grandchildren. Out of respect and love for her, I won't share the full truth of her story here. Suffice it to say, she deserved better.

I learned more about turning suffering into compassion through my dear friend Saul. He lived in the United States for many years but lost his green card. We searched for his family online and spent hours researching and trying to locate phone numbers or any connection to his family in Mexico. It was futile. I even went with him to the Mexican Consulate and the Immigration Department to get his records to replace his green card. Sadly, that was just after the horrific terrorist attack on September 11, 2001. It was difficult for anyone to enter the building, let alone secure paperwork to prove identity. He finally gave up trying to reunite with his family.

Some years later, Saul lost both of his legs just above the knees in a train accident. He had such an amazing faith and stubbornness about him, and I cared deeply for him. I held his hand in the intensive care unit, begging him not to die. Homeless guests, volunteers, and staff gathered to pray for him.

Saul was in the hospital for quite some time after his accident, and I visited him frequently. One day, I rang the buzzer for the ICU nurse to unlock the door and let me in. Saul was sitting up in his bed talking on the phone, laughing and crying at the same time. When he hung up, he told me very excitedly that he was talking with his brother. I was dumbfounded! "How did you find him?"

"A woman with brown hair came into my room and handed me these phone numbers." He held up the tiny piece of yellow paper to show me the phone numbers. I asked who the woman was and he said, "I don't know her name, but she had brown hair and was just here a few minutes ago. She told me she was a friend of yours."

Of course, I was very happy for Saul, but I was also curious. I stopped at the nurse's desk in the ICU before I left the hospital and asked them about the woman with the brown hair. They both looked confused. The nurse on duty for the previous twelve hours said, "No one was allowed in the ICU to visit Saul today, except you." It was a mystery as to how Saul was able to reunite with his brothers and speak with his mother in Mexico. Our God is still a God of miracles today. Always believe in miracles!

Saul gave the shirt off his back if he saw someone suffering. More than once, he gave away his food when one of his friends was hungry. I am certain the compassion Saul had for others in need was his own suffering transformed into compassion by God.

Saul lived just a couple more years. As he got closer to his death, he told me he didn't want me to help him anymore and pushed me out of his life completely. I didn't know where he was when I received a call in the middle of the night from a convalescent home. Saul left my name and phone number as "next of kin," and I arranged for his memorial service and funeral. I also connected with his three brothers, his sister, and his mother in Mexico. I stayed in contact with them and spoke to his brother after a recent major earthquake in Mexico.

The pastor of the church where Grace House was for five of those twelve years, left the church. I reached out to him and wished him well in his new endeavor. Unforgiveness is poison to the soul. I don't want poison in my life. I want to let go of my resentment and pain. God told us to give freely because we have freely received. Jesus died to forgive me for my sins, and so I must freely offer forgiveness to those who sin against me. The pastor sent me a text and told me he would contact me at the end of October. It is now a year later and I have not heard from him. One cannot make another person apologize for the wrongs they have committed. We can't offer forgiveness to others on our own. However, God can soften or change our hearts to both repent and forgive.

I learned the hard way that a support network is crucial to success in any endeavor, especially if you don't have a champion or cheerleader beside you in a relationship. I was single for the majority of the years I ran the homeless ministry and was used to doing things on my own. There were times when the ministry became very challenging. I visited homeless guests in the hospital and held funerals and memorial services for more homeless men and women than I care to count. Out of my own grief and stress, I vented and shared with the wrong person in the wrong way and learned a tough lesson by doing so.

Life can be challenging. Jesus reminds us that we (the church) are to be "one body." We must strengthen our relationships and share honestly and truthfully with one another, never hiding our motives. We must be authentic and real. Only then can we build a positive, trustworthy support network. It was a long road, but I have finally come to terms with the loss of the homeless ministry God birthed.

There was more loss in my family of origin. My half-brother Joe was on my mind as I wrote this book. I located him and his sister through social media. I did not want to interject myself into their lives, although I did extend an invitation. They have chosen not to communicate with me. That's okay; I understand. My prayer for them is they not live in fear, but in faith and love. Although I would like to get to know my half-brother, I don't need to. They have their lives and I have mine. Some relationships, as I said, move on or end.

There are no more searches and no more relatives I need to find. I have come home to myself. Dan and I have found a church with authentic people who know what it means to worship God. We simply love God and let God love us right back. That is what church is supposed to be. There is no need for fancy programs or agendas or a printed list of how the service should go. We worship God in an environment that allows Holy Spirit to live and breathe freely and we are blessed.

Today I received an email from a young woman who said she was searching for her birth father. She says he was homeless and that his name is Saul. My heart skips a beat at the mystery of God in the full circle of life.

Epilogue

*T*S. Eliot once said, "We shall not cease from exploration, and the end of all our exploring will be to arrive where we started and know the place for the first time. The real voyage of discovery consists not in seeking new landscapes, but in having new eyes."

God has given me new eyes. I am humbly grateful and immensely blessed to have spent a good portion of my career in the presence of individuals struggling with homelessness. Saul's dream was a confirmation of God's purpose in my life.

God transformed my suffering into compassion through the challenging and painful times. I have shared God's love, compassion, and encouragement with hurting friends and family, students, survivors of abuse, domestic violence victims, homeless individuals, and God's children wounded by the church. Everything I have endured or experienced is a stepping-stone of transformation on my journey and I am grateful. First Thessalonians 5:18 says, "Give thanks in all circumstances; for this is God's will for you in Christ Jesus."

Acknowledgements

G od, you are the air I breathe. To *my husband Dan* and *my amazing son and daughter*…you are my heartbeat. To *my sister Gayle*, we have a bond that no one can break. To *my parents* and *my sister Betty Jo*, thank you for always being there for me. Many thanks to my friends *Carol* and *Charlene* for encouraging me to be true to myself in writing my story. I am deeply and humbly grateful to my spiritual companion and friend *David Burnet*, who has walked beside me on this journey.

Thanks also to my ever-patient editor *Debra L. Butterfield,* and to my writing group members, *Dr. Leal Abbott* and *Dr. Gwendolyn Kaltoff.*

To all my dear friends who have traveled with me on this journey, thank you for your love and support. And especially to you, *my darling granddaughters,* you are the apple of God's eye…and of mine. I love you so much!

Endnotes

1. "About Krishna." About Krishna | Krishna.com, www.krishna.com/info/about-krishna.

2. Miller Ed.D, Church, & Poole

3. Desmond, "Interview with Mother Teresa: Pencil in the Hand of God," 1989

4. Aigner, H. (1980) *Faint trails: An Introduction to the Fundamentals of Adult Adoptee/Birth parent Reunification Searches* (Western States Ed.) Greenbrae, CA: Paradigm Press.

5. Newman, Louise: https://theconversation.com/do-trauma-victims-really-repress-memories-and-can-therapy-induce-false-memories-84998

6. *American Expose Series: Rituals of Rebellion,* Word Inc. 1993 ISBN:0849984475

7. Ryder, Daniel. *Cover-up of the Century: Satanic Ritual Crime and World Conspiracy.* Ryder Pub., 1996. p. 129-131

8. Thompson, Marjorie J. et al. *Companions in Christ: A Small Group Experience in Spiritual Formation.* Upper Room Books. 2001. p.241

About the Author

*C*indy Burger is an author, founder of a Christian homeless ministry, and a spiritual director with HolyListening.com. Her most treasured title is "Grandma." She adores her three adult children and four precious granddaughters. Cindy and her husband live in California where they serve as "staff" for their large Maine Coon cat.

You can reach her at CLBurgerLullaby@gmail.com.

If you enjoyed this book, will you
consider sharing it with others?

- Please mention the book on Facebook, Twitter, Pinterest, or your blog.
- Recommend this book to your small group, book club, and workplace.
- Pick up a copy for someone you know who would be challenged or encouraged by the message.
- Write a review on Amazon.com, BN.com or Goodreads.com

Made in the USA
San Bernardino, CA
02 April 2020